Rising Above

Empowering Stories of Women Overcoming Adversity

Alison Maloni

Copyright © 2025 Alison Maloni

www.alisonmaycommunications.com

All rights reserved. No part of this book may be used or reproduced by any means, graphic, electronic, or mechanical, including photocopying, recording, taping or by any information storage retrieval system without the written permission of the publisher except in the case of brief quotations embodied in critical articles and reviews.

Because of the dynamic nature of the Internet, any web addresses or links contained in this book may have changed since publication and may no longer be valid. The views expressed in this work are solely those of the author and do not necessarily reflect the views of the publisher, and the publisher hereby disclaims any responsibility for them.

Cover image by Kladyk from Getty Images

Any people depicted in stock imagery provided by Getty Images are models, and such images are being used for illustrative purposes only.

Prepared for publication by www.40DayPublishing.com

Cover design by Tiffany Gallen

Printed in the United States of America

Table of Contents

Foreword i

Introduction iii

Dedication v

Chapter 1 She Would Have Stayed 1

Chapter 2 Trust Your Gut 11

Chapter 3 Wounded Warrior 21

Chapter 4 You are Not Too Much 33

Chapter 5 37 Days in Jail 39

Chapter 6 Choose Love 49

Chapter 7 You are Worthy 63

Chapter 8 Never Give Up 75

Chapter 9 Love Yourself 87

Chapter 10 You are Enough 97

Conclusion 108

Acknowledgments 109

Foreword

Alison Maloni's book *Rising Above* touches upon the heartstrings of our souls. These stories illuminate the dynamic cultivatable virtues in life: hope, faith, strength, courage, and love interwoven magically to let us arrive at the lesson of it all. For where there is love, there is always a way forward to turn our pain into a purpose far greater than we ever imagined. In a world so enchanted by social media, Allison has pulled back the veil to enrich our lives with authentic stories that remind us never to give up!

Rising Above is filled with thought-provoking truths unimaginable that anyone could survive, yet these women thrive. After reading these remarkable stories, I pray that you feel as empowered and inspired as I did. They will stay with you always, and when in doubt, I hope you will think of these incredible women and remember if they can do it, so can you because the answers already lie within you. I love this book! It is a must read for anyone who needs a beacon of light in their lives!

JJ Phillips M.A.
Author, advocate, creative

Introduction

In every corner of the globe, women are battling unseen wars. From the depths of personal tragedy to the heights of societal impact, they are scripting narratives of resilience, courage, and transformation. This book is a testament to that power brought to life through the stories of remarkable women who have faced formidable challenges and emerged stronger for themselves and others. Their narratives are harrowing and inspiring, offering hope and strength to all who read them. This book is more than a collection of stories; it's a tribute to the indomitable spirit of women everywhere. It's a rallying cry for those who feel alone in their battles and a confirmation that even in the most desperate times, one can find the strength to rise, fight, and make a difference.

The women in this book are brave enough to speak up and share their stories. For some, it's their first time going public with their journey.

One woman found herself in an abusive relationship—a situation too many know, and yet few escape. She was forced to do things she never imagined. She would do blaming herself if her fiancé was upset. She believed she had to be the perfect woman in the relationship. If she questioned him, he would give her the silent treatment. And if she spoke up, he would threaten her safety. Many women don't realize they are in relationships with narcissists before it's too late. They trust these men, marry them and even stay with them. However, unexpected turns in life can rescue those women from despair.

RISING ABOVE

Consider the bravery of a mother whose son was killed in the Sandy Hook school shooting. He performed heroic acts that day. Her life changed irrevocably, but she chooses to honor his memory by advocating for change channeling her sorrow into a force for good.

Another woman was young, healthy, and successful but her body was fighting its own battle. One doctor after the next told her she was fine. If she listened to their advice she might not be here today.

Others have battled personal demons and physical afflictions. A successful business owner in the fitness industry survived a devastating motorcycle accident enduring the agonizing reality of a life-changing experience that tested her in every way.

Imagine being a public figure in a small city. One minute you are filming a TV series on parenting. Then, in what seems like a flash, you are sitting in a jail cell for a crime you didn't commit.

Consider the stories from a human trafficking survivor, those battling severe depression, a couple who became homeless, and many more women who share their personal journeys.

As you turn these pages, may you find the courage to see your struggles anew, draw strength from these incredible women, and know you are not alone.

Since I was nine, I've wanted to share stories about people facing challenges. People impacted by life-changing catastrophes who chose to rise above circumstances to make a difference. And finally, stories that haven't been told yet because of fear.

Our voices are powerful, and sometimes, we only have our voice to make an impact.

To every woman who has ever doubted her strength, questioned her worth, or feared the future—this book is for you. It is a celebration of courage in the face of unimaginable trials and a reminder that even in our darkest moments, we can find a way to light the path ahead. Welcome to a journey of resilience, empowerment, and transformation.

Dedication

This book is dedicated to Darlene Shortridge Mawhinney. This book and my previous one wouldn't have been possible without her.

I met Darlene through a Facebook women's group when I began writing Breaking in the News. Build Buzz for Your Brand. She was the co-owner of 40 Day Publishing. After talking to her for ten minutes, I immediately connected with her. Her care for me was genuine. Darlene was interested in what I was writing about, and we began working together. I followed her on social media and saw the true love of her family, faith, and business. When I pondered writing my second book, I reached out to Darlene to see what she thought about my concept. In her upbeat, positive voice, she said, "That is such a great idea. I can't wait to read it."

Not long after that conversation, I learned Darlene unexpectedly passed away. She was too young and had so much life to live with her family and friends. She, too, had a story. Fortunately, her husband, Dan Mawhinney shared it with me in full. In this book, you will read about the rocky road she navigated early in life, and how her love for God and family kept her on the right path. Darlene was, and still is, the true definition of positivity.

Darlene, I am forever grateful for your belief in me and the opportunity to share your story. Dan, your willingness to open up about Darlene's life and legacy is a testament to your love and strength. I am honored to have been entrusted with this task.

Katie Mares

Chapter 1
She Would Have Stayed

*"I can be changed by what happens to me.
But I refuse to be reduced by it."*

- Maya Angelou

When I interviewed Katie Mares for this book in August 2023, an immediate connection formed. She was a single mom, an entrepreneur, a speaker, and a powerful storyteller. I knew her story of resilience and wise decisions would have an impact on many women.

Katie grew up in a home where both of her parents were addicts and largely absent. From a very young age she took on the roles of mother, sister, chef, tutor, and caregiver for her younger brother and sister. Most nights she stayed up late to watch over her father, who sat in a chair with a drink in one hand and a cigar in the other making sure he didn't accidentally burn the house down. Katie's childhood was spent in constant protection of her siblings.

At nineteen she was kicked out of her house. Shortly afterward, she met the man who became her husband. They had two beautiful children together, but Katie described the marriage as loveless and abusive. It took her fifteen years to finally leave—a decision she made for the sake of her children—wanting them to thrive in a healthier environment.

Following her divorce, Katie reentered the dating scene—a daunting prospect for many post-divorcees. After dating a few "frogs," as she put it, she thought she had finally found her prince. For the first time in a long while, she felt like she was on track to have the life she had always dreamed of. It didn't take long before her new boyfriend proposed.

Newly engaged, Katie hoped she could now show her children what a loving relationship truly looked like. On the surface, it seemed as though the pieces of her life were finally falling into place.

That was what I had planned on writing about. The hard choices she made and the resilience of her being a single mom. But before I began writing this book, her life took a dramatic turn. And now, this is Katie's story.

Katie finally found her fairytale life. She traveled, found the man of her dreams, created a blended family, wore a beautiful ring, and planned a destination wedding. In other words, it was that happily-ever-after she dreamed of. But what appeared on social media, and even what friends heard, didn't reflect what was really happening behind closed doors.

"I told you that everything was great," Katie recalled. "I had fallen in love. I was getting married. I made it out of one situation and lived my best life. But I completely fabricated that best life."

So why tell everyone her life was great? Katie says she desperately wanted everything she portrayed to be real. She didn't want this relationship to fail too. Katie was scared and living in darkness. Like thousands of women, she stayed silent. On the outside, she smiled and pretended her life was perfect. But inside, she was dying.

For women and men who have not gone through an abusive relationship, the number one question victims receive is, "Why did you stay? Why not leave?" According to the National Family Health Survey, 77% of women who are in relationships of domestic abuse stay silent.

Katie says she wishes it was that simple. She wished she could have said she was done, packed up, and start a new life. But there's much more to the psychology behind it.

"I wore a three-and-a-half-carat diamond ring, traveled the world, worked for his businesses, and even invested in them," said Katie. "But then there's the fear of financial abandonment and you start thinking, 'My life seems good—how dare I believe it's really this bad?'

Katie, like many who have been in relationships with narcissists, internalized the blame. She thought if she could just improve herself, things would get better. She believed, "If I work on myself and show up as the best version of me, maybe it will be enough. And if it's not, I'll read more books, go to counseling, do everything I can."

And that's exactly what she did. Katie threw herself into therapy, read every book she could find, listened to podcasts, smiled on the outside while crying on the inside, spent hours at the gym, and tried everything to maintain the image of perfection.

In therapy, Katie opened completely, hoping to gain tools to cope with the abuse. Though her therapist warned her the situation wasn't right or sustainable, he agreed to support her and help her stay as mentally healthy as possible if she chose to remain in the relationship. Katie says she knew this wasn't the best way to deal with this verbally abusive relationship. She was determined to marry her fiancé and deal with this new normal.

Katie had come to understand the insidious way narcissists manipulate everything around them. Narcissists always positioned themselves at the center of attention. They had a way of isolating their partners from friends and family, demanding the focus be entirely on them. In their mind, their world was the only one that mattered. If a partner had children, the narcissist expected her to uproot the children to be closer to him. If she had a job, he would pressure her to quit and work for him instead. As for friends,—the narcissist had to be the only "necessary" companion in his partner's life, or he would convince her his friends were far superior to hers

Katie recounted a time when she should have been celebrating her accomplishment of delivering a TED Talk. However, her fiancé ruined that special moment. What's important to note is that this sabotage started before she gave her speech.

Katie poured endless hours into preparing for her TED Talk. In the days leading up to it, she faced relentless criticism from her fiancé. He accused her of being too focused on the talk fueling her anxiety and making her feel awful. On the night of her big speech, he showed up in the audience. Katie, completely drained from both the preparation and emotional strain wanted to go to bed after the event. Instead, he made a cutting remark, saying, "You haven't seen me in two weeks. You've been with your kids and working. You say you want to be my fantasy, but you're not."

It was at that point Katie says the verbal abuse turned physical.

"I finally gathered the courage to tell him he could be abusive," Katie recalled. "In that moment, he shoved me down onto the bed so hard I could feel his fingers digging into my ribcage. 'Is this abuse?' he asked. He knocked me down again as I tried to get up, repeating, 'Is this abuse?'"

Shaking and crying, Katie mustered all her strength to get up. The moment she stood, she said he pushed her down repeating the abuse question. Every time she was pushed down, she got up. Like many women in abusive relationships, she changed her tone and apologized for making him upset.

"I said I'm so sorry. I'll be better. Just love me. I'm sorry. I'm sorry. I'm sorry."

After hours of tears, Katie finally fell asleep. When she woke and saw the light of the morning creep through the windows the realization of what happened the night before sunk in. But, you would never know it by how her fiancé acted.

After every episode of abuse, the love bombing began. Like clockwork, Katie says her fiancé would send her texts telling her how amazing she was and encouraged her to keep moving forward. He'd tell her how lucky he was to have her and how he could see she truly wanted to be everything for him. Those messages would temporarily make Katie feel special, pulling her back into the cycle, making her believe that maybe things could get better.

But they didn't. Katie walked on eggshells twenty-four-seven.

The abuse cycle worsened. Katie was broken mentally and physically.

Katie reached a point where her depression became so overwhelming that even the smallest tasks felt like victories. She found herself celebrating simple things like eating or managing to take a shower. Waking up each day and taking care of her kids became monumental achievements, marking how deeply she was struggling.

She recounts one time when she went to see her fiancé. Things got so bad she feared for her life.

"He straddled me and beat himself with my hands," Katie recounted. "He took my hands by my wrist and beat himself with my hands so hard he fractured a bone in my hand."

Few people knew about the abuse, but Katie began opening up to people who were close to her. One such person was her fiancé's daughter.

Shortly after she shared what was happening with the daughter, the daughter told her dad. That is when Katie says he ended everything.

Since Katie and her fiancé planned on joining households through marriage, they had been sharing bank accounts and investments. Once the relationship ended, he made sure Katie couldn't access anything. He locked her out of the bank account. Within twenty-four hours, her credit cards were canceled.

Katie was left in debt, including the $306,000 she lent him. She had no access to money or her assets. She lost everything.

Katie remembered that moment all too well. He told her to sell her body for groceries because, in his words, she was "good at it." And like many abused women, she did what she thought she had to—she made excuses for him. She convinced herself she was the problem. Katie gaslit her own mind into believing if she could just be better, they would be better

But they weren't better and they weren't going to get better. Sometimes, a higher power pulls you out of a situation in which you feel stuck. Katie thanked God for His intervention because like many abused women, she would have stayed.

"I would have married him, Katie said. "I would've stayed. I would've endured. The abuse felt normal. I would have rather endured the volatility (his and mine) for his love and the quiet moments in which I rested my head on his chest."

RISING ABOVE

As Katie tried to put her life back together, she knew other women and men experienced similar situations. She was determined to do something to help others. That's when Ladies Take Control was born. LTC is a community app—an educational safe space for people to grow and develop. Despite self-doubt, Katie is resolute in becoming a beacon of hope for others and fostering a supportive community.

The free app, personal and professional development events, and community serves as a lifeline for women who have been silenced, oppressed, and rendered powerless by abuse.

Ladies Take Control offers a comprehensive array of accessible resources, including courses, masterminds, coaching, and spiritual guidance. Daily inspirations and community chats facilitate continuous personal development and support for women on their journey toward empowerment and healing. Katie has had two successful virtual conferences and plans to have an in-person event next.

Katie was one of the 14% of women who decide to say something about her situation by launching Ladies Take Control, but it didn't come without consequences.

Speaking out unleashed a torrent of threats, extortion, and harassment against Katie. He former fiancé did everything in his power to silence her. While she anticipated he would be upset, she never imagined it would escalate to this level. The intensity of his retaliation took her by surprise.

Katie says narcissistic abuse is what makes it difficult for women to believe they are making the right decision to leave. Narcissists will make you think you are crazy. They claim you are overreacting and lying. They convince you that you are the bad person in the relationship when, in fact, it is them. After speaking publicly about her relationship, Katie said the mental games started again when he contacted her. She questioned herself.

"I was going back through all the text messages and journal entries from the past," Katie recalled. "He made me question myself. It was so hard that my suicidal thoughts came back. I was tired of it being hard."

Tired but determined and despite the threats, Katie kept moving forward.

She came to understand that helping other men and women in abusive relationships was her calling. The feedback she's received from men who listen to her story has been nothing short of beautiful. They shared their own stories revealing how they've faced similar struggles and emotions. Katie says that It's become clear to her that abuse isn't a struggle exclusive to women. Men are often silenced and suffer in their own way.

Katie received countless phone calls and text messages from people who felt deeply moved by her words. "I felt like you were speaking directly to me," some of them said. Often they were grown men whose voices broke with emotion. Every time she got a message from someone—whether a man or a woman—it became her lifeline. It reminded her why she was doing this. Even if she was helping just one person, it made everything she was going through worthwhile.

Since Katie continued to receive threats from her ex, she was tempted to go back to being quiet and let someone else speak up. But she believes she was given this mission to help change the lives of others.

"God is who keeps me going," said Katie. "I truly believe that I was given this situation so I could help change the lives of others. I believe He blessed me with incredible gifts—the ability to be articulate, the ability to stay positive, and the strength I wear like armor. I feel like these are gifts He gave me from birth. I have a voice and I need to use it. I need to break the silence."

Breaking the silence helped Katie with the healing process. In addition to therapy, reading scriptures, and following Instagram reels that motivate her, Katie says anyone going through this needs to surround themselves with a group of people who are honest and encouraging. There's no better resource than those who love you and can tell you things a therapist can't.

One day, one of Katie's friends looked her straight in the eyes, her expression serious and full of concern. "Katie," she said firmly, "I will never judge you. But if you go back, I'm done. Because I can't save you." The weight of those words hung in the air—a stark reminder of the danger Katie was in and the limits of even the closest friendships.

Katie took control of her life and is now helping others do the same through Ladies Take Control. She is also working on her third book, which will help more victims of abuse. Healing takes a long time. Every day is a challenge—sometimes brutal. Every day, Katie reminds herself she might not be alive today if she didn't get out.

"I don't want another woman to suffer if they don't have to. If that means I must fight harder, I will. I will never give up."

Resources

- Domestic Violence Hotline https://www.thehotline.org/stakeholders/domestic-violence-statistics/
- LadiesTakeControl.com
- KatieMares.com

Samantha Harris

Chapter 2

Trust Your Gut

"If you do have a mastectomy, it doesn't make you any less of a woman. You are still beautiful; you are still amazing. You're still powerful."

-Christinia Applegate

Samantha Harris was a fit, healthy working mom. She stood on the red carpet interviewing the stars of Hollywood living out her dreams and loving life. On the dawn of her fortieth birthday, Samantha knew it was time to get a mammogram. Especially considering her dad died of colon cancer at the age of fifty and her grandmother was a breast cancer survivor. Because of this, Samantha had cancer on her radar.

The proactive mom got a mammogram and received the news everyone wanted to hear: 'It's clear.'

With that in the rear-view mirror, she continued with her busy life until eleven days later.

"I was changing," Samantha recalled. "You know how those sports bras are so constricting. So, you take them off, and you kind of move the girls to the left and the right—you do a little rotation. It was then I felt this lump."

Pulse racing, Samantha called her OBGYN because she knew and trusted this doctor. She had been seeing the doctor since she was in her twenties. Fortunately, an appointment was made for the near future.

Two days later, she went in for the exam. Her doctor didn't seem too concerned and told her lumps were typical in forty-year-old breasts. Since the mammogram was clear, she shouldn't worry.

But there was something in Samantha's mind telling her something was wrong.

A month later, the lump was still there, and her gut told her to get a second opinion. Samantha called her internist. They did a check, and once again, Samantha was told nothing was wrong and sent on her way.

Now what?

Samantha had two doctors tell her she was fine.

Four months went by since she first discovered the lump. Her inner voice screamed louder and louder something was wrong.

"It was saying, 'Samantha, if you're going to live with this 'nothing' lump, then shouldn't you know what's happening inside that lump before you agree to live with it?'"

Samantha's journey wasn't just about trusting her gut; it was also about listening to the voices of those around her who cared deeply. She had an inner voice telling her to push forward and seek another opinion. In addition, her mom constantly asked, "Is that lump still there? What is it doing? Why haven't they checked it again?"

Samantha's stepdad, a surgeon, joined in, adding another layer of urgency. With these voices all coming at her from different directions, she knew she had to act. It was a team of caring voices—her own, her mom's, and her stepdad's that pushed her to take a crucial step of getting a third opinion.

Finally, Samantha made an appointment at St. John's Hospital Breast Center in Santa Monica, California.

She felt odd seeing an oncologist who specialized in treating women for breast cancer. According to the two doctors she had seen, she didn't have cancer.

Samantha remembered sitting in the waiting room looking at the other women wondering if they had cancer.

During that appointment she had two ultrasounds and a needle biopsy. The oncologist told her she wasn't crazy. Finally, someone listened to her. The doctor said she saw something. But Samantha was again told it doesn't look like cancer.

Relief!

When the needle biopsy results came back a week later, the doctor told Samantha to bring her husband to the appointment. In the best-case scenario, Samantha and her husband could leave after she saw her and have a nice lunch together.

In the case of unpleasant news, the doctor wanted to make sure she had her husband's support.

Samantha and her husband sat in the exam office nerves abuzz. The doctor said she had good news and bad news. The good news was that the lump wasn't cancer. The bad news was that she didn't know what it was. The doctor recommended doing a lumpectomy. Afterward, the tissue would be sent to a lab for further examination and testing.

Relief!

Samantha and her husband had a celebratory lunch. Third time was a charm. It absolutely was not cancer.

Samantha underwent the lumpectomy assured it wasn't cancer. Even the MRI she had going into surgery did not detect cancer. It was just an annoying lump that was now gone. She could move on.

When the pathology report was ready for pick up, Samantha told her husband he didn't need to go with her. Time and time again, the results were negative. No cancer.

"I mean, gosh, how many people, how many times do you want to be dragged to someone else's doctor's appointment. I didn't even want to go to my appointment."

Samantha sat alone in the doctor's office, knowing she'd hear everything was fine.

But it was not.

Samantha's world shifted in an instant when the doctor delivered the news. The words "carcinoma" and "ductal carcinoma in situ" felt foreign, like a language she didn't quite understand. But deep down, she knew exactly what those words meant—breast cancer.

RISING ABOVE

As Samantha sat in the doctor's office, the moment felt surreal. The doctor drew diagrams marking dots to show where the tumor was located. Information came at her so quickly—one medical term after another—that it felt overwhelming. In the midst of it all, she struggled to process everything. All she could grasp in that moment was one undeniable fact: I have cancer.

After telling her husband the news, Samantha read everything she could about the disease. She also took her pathology report to another radiologist for a second opinion. That doctor agreed with the first, so it was now a matter of treatment plans.

Samantha learned at the beginning of her journey to get multiple opinions. Within a week and a half, she had seen three surgical oncologists. She had two paths she could take.

She could have another lumpectomy to get clear margins, followed by thirty rounds of radiation over six weeks. Or she could have a single or double mastectomy which was much more invasive.

Samantha carefully weighed her options seeking guidance from as many doctors and breast cancer survivors as she could. She asked them thoughtful, probing questions. "What surgery and treatment plan did you choose? How do you feel about that decision? What were the pros and cons? What was your reason for making that choice?" Each conversation helped her piece together the best path forward.

Samantha realized the more information she gathered, the clearer her path became. By immersing herself in research, seeking opinions, and understanding her options, she was able to make decisions that were right for her. Filling herself with as much knowledge as possible put her in a stronger position to take control of her situation and act with confidence.

After hours of consultations and education, Samantha decided she was going to do a double mastectomy. The cancer already had spread to one lymph node. Out of precaution, all eleven lymph nodes were taken out.

In addition to the surgery, her doctors told her she could benefit from four rounds of chemotherapy in addition to the radiation. Studies showed a twenty percent chance of cancer coming back without radiation treatments.

Samantha brought that study to one of her doctors and was told the radiation recommendation was correct—up until a few weeks prior. Two studies had come out figuring in tumor size. The doctor told Samantha her tumors were small. According to this new study, radiation wouldn't make a difference.

In the eleventh hour, Samantha chose not to do radiation and chemo.

Samantha's oncologist told her she was in a gray area when it came to chemotherapy. Completing four rounds would reduce her chance of recurrence by one to four percent. She remembered replying, "I want to weigh what chemo might do to me and the potential long-term effects. I need to feel very confident in that decision." There were days when she questioned whether it was the right choice. Overall, she felt at peace with it. After her cancer diagnosis, Samantha made significant lifestyle changes she hadn't realized were within her control—steps to reduce her risk and regain a sense of power over her health.

Once the surgeries were over, the hard part was recovery. Samantha was used to exercising every day and being an active mom. Now, she was in her bed for three weeks after each operation. She could only get out of bed for twenty minutes every two hours.

Used to being busy, Samantha used her down time to do research.

"I worked like crazy on my computer," Samantha recalled. "I stayed as busy as possible to keep my mind occupied. I'm someone who's always on the go, so waiting six weeks after each surgery to get back to anything beyond a slow walk around the block was incredibly hard for me."

Samantha says it was a wake-up call—realizing the profound impact exercise had on her mental health. She began to feel a shift, but at the time, she had no idea how much it would transform her outlook. It wasn't about staying physically fit anymore; it became about her "why"—the deeper purpose behind why she exercised. That shift in perspective completely changed the way she approached her routine and her life.

Samantha says true health and wellness didn't come into clear focus until three, four, or five years after her diagnosis when she started to shift into wellness and became a certified health coach. She learned her previous ideas about health were inaccurate.

Samantha always believed she was healthy. She was the type to eat egg white omelets, cheese-free pizza, and skinless chicken breasts loading up on as much animal protein as possible. In her mind, fat was the enemy, something to avoid at all costs. She thought she exercised because she needed to look good. She wanted to look good, and more than anything, she wanted to look strong. It wasn't until later she realized how narrow her definition of health had been.

After Samantha began healing, she dove deep into studying health and wellness. She looked at everything from what we put in and on our bodies, to how we exercise.

She became a National Ambassador for Susan G. Komen. She learned only 5-10% of breast cancer is genetic.

Samantha had always assumed her cancer was hereditary, especially with a family history of the disease. When she found out it wasn't, she admitted feeling disappointed and confused at first, questioning why she developed it. But instead of dwelling on the unknown, she turned to her journalism roots and became a research junkie. Samantha dove into every resource she could find determined to understand more. What she discovered was eye-opening: the things we put on and around our bodies significantly impact our overall health. That realization fueled her journey toward healing and making more informed choices.

After looking at hundreds of pages of research, Samantha was empowered.

"I thought, okay, this happened," Samantha said. "I can make changes, I can have some power, I can take back control of my well-being."

She systematically started making small, impactful changes from how she ate, to her exercise approach. She examined the products she used on and around her body. She analyzed household cleaners, makeup, and skincare. In addition, she factored in stress and sleep.

Samantha says that her holistic approach was eye-opening, but she couldn't find one book that had all the answers she was looking for. That's how her book, Your Healthiest Healthy, came to be.

Samantha realized how much work all the research had been. Most people simply didn't have the time for. That was why she decided to write the book—to share all the knowledge she had gathered with others making it easier for them to access the information that had taken her so long to compile.

Samantha expanded well beyond the book. She went back to school to became a certified health coach.

She now shares her knowledge in social media posts, coaching sessions, online courses, retreats, and membership communities.

This is a path that Samantha never saw in her future.

"When I was little, my dream job was to be on TV," Samantha said. "I hoped I could be like Barbara Walters one day. I was just a twelve-year-old girl from Minnesota, but I dreamed of being in front of the camera."

While she did achieve her dream of being in front of camera as an Emmy-winning television host, including co-hosting Dancing with the Stars and serving as a correspondent and weekend anchor for shows like Entertainment Tonight and The Insider. Samantha says she loves this new direction in life. She is now helping thousands of women and men find health, learn why exercise is important, and trust their gut.

Samantha reflected on her decision, "Thank goodness I listened to that voice in my head and pursued it." She felt a deep sense of gratitude for her persistence, adding, "I am so happy I kept asking and pushing." For her it was a reminder we can't afford to ignore what's important. "We can't stick our heads in the sand," she emphasized. Samantha knew the value of advocacy, especially when it came to health matters. "And if we're lucky enough to have insurance that allows multiple opinions, we should get multiple opinions." It was a lesson in perseverance and taking control of her own well-being.

After being cancer-free for ten years, Samantha Harris received devastating news she never thought she'd hear again. In August 2024, she learned her breast cancer returned. With her characteristic courage,

Samantha shared the news with her followers on Instagram. The recurrence was in the same location as the original lump from 2014, but this time, she caught it early thanks to her vigilance.

Determined to approach the diagnosis head-on, Samantha documented her journey on social media, providing her followers with an inside look at what she was going through. Following her doctor's recommendation, she underwent a partial mastectomy. Throughout her battle, she continued to share her experience offering guidance, research, and unwavering support to those facing similar challenges. Her goal remained to help people achieve a healthier lifestyle even while navigating her own difficult path.

Samantha firmly believes that the health choices she made over the years, including her commitment to fitness and nutrition, helped slow the cancer's growth and mitigate its spread. Remarkably, just two weeks after her surgery, she was back to exercising. She knows how crucial physical activity is for overall health and recovery. Through it all, she remained an inspiration, showing her followers the power of perseverance and the importance of taking control of one's health.

Samantha often found herself returning to the simple, yet profound advice: "Just please, eat vegetables. Start now. Eat all the colors!" It was more than just a casual reminder; it was a principle deeply ingrained in her, passed down from her mother, who always told her to eat her veggies. But it wasn't just about the food. For Samantha, this mantra symbolized her entire journey—a testament to her tenacity in chasing what she wanted and never accepting no as an answer. She pursued her dreams relentlessly, and in the end, she was beyond grateful for that unwavering determination. It's a lesson she carries with her to this day, one she eagerly passes on to others. Whether it's about health or ambition, Samantha believes you must take charge and push forward, no matter the odds.

Samantha's Non-Negotiables

Exercise:

She says she will exercise every day. She will work hard to move her body.

Food:

She fuels her body with nourishing food every day with items such as a smoothie, to ensure she gets whole food ingredients in her system.

Be kind to Yourself:

She reminds herself to be kinder and not beat herself up for the seventeen things she didn't finish. She reframes her situation to celebrate the twenty things she did get done.

Samantha's number one advice for women is to listen to their body and gut.

She reflected on how easy it is to dismiss things, particularly for women who are constantly juggling so many responsibilities.

"I think when we just write things off, it's because we're so often stretched thin." As women, we tend to place themselves last on our own to-do lists. We always prioritize everything and everyone else before ourselves. This was a reality she knew all too well—a cycle that was easy to fall into but hard to break.

Prioritizing self-care as selfless instead of selfish allows us to take better care of ourselves. Samantha said If we aren't caring for ourselves, we can't care for those around us.

If Samantha had not done that, she might not be here today.

Resources

- https://samantha-harris.com/
- Susan G Komen
- https://www.komen.org/

Rebecca Kiessling

Caleb and Kyler Kiessling

Chapter 3
Wounded Warrior

"I would have wanted someone to have warned me. The government's number one role is to protect us and they failed. My sons deserved to be protected.'

- Rebecca Kiessling

These were the anguished words of Rebecca Kiessling, a mother whose world was shattered by the opioid crisis. A crisis that took both of her sons, Caleb and Kyler, in one devastating blow. The nightmare began with a single pill—one laced with deadly fentanyl. Her story isn't about personal blame, but systemic failure.

"I never would have thought my sons would fall victim to this," recalled Rebecca. "We always talked openly about the dangers of drugs."

Yet the reality of the drug trade evolved faster than any parent could anticipate. Fentanyl, a synthetic opioid fifty to one-hundred times more potent than morphine, has infiltrated even the most unsuspecting corners of society masquerading as harmless prescription pills and street drugs alike.

Rebecca, like every parent, did everything possible to protect her children.

For Rebecca, her adopted sons were even more precious because she was adopted. Raised by loving parents, she understood the unique love adoption creates—a bond transcending bloodlines. So, when Rebecca became a mother to Caleb and Kyler, her love for them was unwavering, fierce, and protective.

"They weren't just my sons—they were my miracle," Rebecca explained. "We chose each other. We became a family in the truest sense of the word."

It took a while to become a whole family as Rebecca first adopted Caleb from his mother who was a drug addict. Kyler wasn't born yet. But the Kiessling house was filling with love. Next, Rebecca and her husband adopted a baby girl named Cassie.

"I have pictures of them together in a crib with Caleb's arm around Cassie's shoulder," Rebecca recalled. "He would stare at her all the time. He was fascinated by her."

But tragedy struck shaking the growing family to the core. Cassie died at thirty-three days old from complications. Rebecca says Caleb was too young to process the loss and took it very hard.

She walked into the kitchen to find him standing on a chair, his little hand pointing toward the ceiling. With innocent eyes, he said he wanted to see Cassie. Her heart swelled with emotion as she knelt beside him, "God has special plans for your life." It was a tender moment filled with the weight of a child's longing and comforting reassurance only a mother could give.

Rebecca always told Caleb to be careful and take care of himself. Birthmother being an addict, Rebecca says she was always worried Caleb would inherit addiction.

Two years passed.

Caleb's birth mother was pregnant again. Rebecca says according to records, she took drugs while pregnant—up until the week Kyler was born. Kyler's father was high on heroin and tried to drown him when he was nine weeks old.

When Rebecca heard about this, she called Child Protective Services hoping to take in Kyler. After months of legal battles, the judge finally approved the adoption of Kyler. Caleb was two and a half, and Kyler just turned one.

"On the drive home, the two of them were sitting there staring at each other and making faces," Rebecca remembered. "I couldn't help but think, Look at them—two brothers. Each one so unique in his own way." It was one of those simple moments that made her heart swell with love and appreciation for their special bond.

Growing up, Caleb was the performer and Kyler was fearless. The boys lived a normal life skateboarding and playing with friends. Rebecca, who grew up with substance abuse in her house, considered the boys' family history. She did everything in her power keep them safe. This included homeschooling. But things changed when her husband wanted the boys to go to a public high school.

During those years in high school, Rebecca said the boys experimented with vaping, marijuana, and pills. No matter what she did, Caleb and Kyler went down a path she tried desperately to stop. She says both boys tried to quit vaping but the withdrawal was horrible.

Rebecca resisted giving her children phones until much later than most. Even then, she made a point of regularly checking them. She kept a close eye on what the boys were doing. When things started to feel off, she didn't hesitate to go to the school and plead with them to shut down troubling behaviors.

Deep down, Rebecca knew something was wrong. Despite all her efforts, her mother's instinct told her there was more beneath the surface.

Caleb eventually admitted he had an addiction to vaping marijuana and pills. With her help, he was able to get clean and went from barely making passing grades to graduate from high school. On the right path, he graduated early with honors, planned to go into the Navy, and scored in the 90th percentile on the PICAT test.

But Caleb never made it into the Navy. He told Rebecca he didn't want to leave his brother because Kyler was still battling addiction.

Then COVID hit and Rebecca said things got tough for her sons. Caleb and Kyler got arrested for attempting to break into a jewelry store. With bail set at $17,000, Rebecca let them stay in jail and get clean. She did not want to be an enabler.

Both Caleb and Kyler called Rebecca from jail and admitted that they need to change. Caleb got involved in Celebrate Recovery while he was in jail. Kyler worked alone on getting himself clean. Rebecca felt optimistic as they were safe and focused on their health.

But their jail time was cut short because of the pandemic and a state-funded program bailed them out. Rebecca pleaded against it because she knew the boys were starting to heal. The judge let them go. He told her Caleb and Kyler would go to rehab. Unfortunately, it wasn't actual rehab. This placement made things worse.

Rebecca recounted the situation, frustration clear in her voice. Caleb and Kyler had been placed in a halfway house located in a drug-infested neighborhood in Pontiac, Michigan. "It wasn't rehab at all," she explained. "Every day, the boys were allowed to leave for walks. During those walks, they had easy access to drugs. It was a stark contrast to the structured environment they expected. It only worsened the situation instead of helping."

Upon leaving the halfway house, the courts ordered the boys to live apart and go to work. Like many during COVID, the boys received checks from the government. There was no need to find jobs immediately since many places were shut down. Caleb and Kyler planned to find jobs when the funds ran out.

Things went from bad to worse.

Rebecca recalled that moment with a mixture of fear and urgency. Her daughter had come to her, saying a friend had seen something troubling on Snapchat—her son had posted pictures of pills. Terrified, she immediately contacted their father, her voice shaking, "You have to take them to rehab." The realization hit her hard. In that moment she knew something had to change before it was too late.

By this time, the boys were over eighteen. They had to enter rehab on their own free will. Caleb and Kyler's dad got a hotel for them and planned on talking to them about rehab the next morning.

"I told Caleb I was so worried about him and he hugged me," Rebecca remembers. "He said he loved me too."

Those were Rebecca's last words to her son.

The next day, July 29, 2020, Rebecca got a call from her now ex-husband.

"He said, 'Are you alone? Are you sitting down?' Recalled Rebecca. "He then told me that both boys were dead. And I just started screaming."

Caleb and Kyler died from fentanyl poisoning. Another person died at the same time. The dealer who sold them the drugs was hospitalized.

The dealer had overdosed a month before. Rebecca alleges he knew he was selling a deadly product. The punishment for killing three people with poisonous drugs was fifteen years in prison. That's all.

Rebecca was consumed by the grief over the loss of both boys. She second-guessed everything she did or didn't do. She went to counseling, joined grief groups, and found Facebook group pages of parents who lost their kids to fentanyl. She prayed, cried, suffered from anxiety, and tried to survive from one day to the next.

Rebecca's three daughters watched in horror as their mother deteriorated before their eyes. The community did what they could to help by setting up a GoFundMe page for the funeral and checking in on Rebecca and her family. They were broken. Could they ever heal and move forward?

Rebecca reflected on that painful time, her voice heavy with emotion. Her daughters were thirteen, fifteen, and seventeen when the boys died. "It was incredibly hard on them," she admitted, her eyes welling up with tears. They didn't get to have the mother they needed during those years because she was consumed by grief, crying all the time. It broke her heart to realize how much her daughters had lost—not only their brothers but also the presence of a fully available mother.

Losing a child changes a person. The grief never leaves. Many say you learn to live with the loss, but you never really do.

Rebecca decided to focus on three things: taking care of her daughters, improving her mental health through exercise—specifically gravel biking, and educating parents about the dangers of fentanyl. Fentanyl was a drug Rebecca never heard of before. Something she wished the police officer told her about when her sons were first arrested.

After the boys died, she unexpectedly ran into the officer who had arrested her sons. The encounter stirred up painful memories. He revealed her sons had been taking Xanax at the time. Desperate for answers she asked, "Do you know about fentanyl?" The officer nodded. She pressed further, "Did you know they put fentanyl in fake Xanax and Percocet?" Again, he said yes. Then she asked if he knew about Narcan, the life-saving antidote. He answered yes. Anger and disbelief welled up inside her. "Well, I didn't!" she exclaimed, her voice shaking. "I didn't know my sons were dabbling in that. Why didn't you warn me? Why didn't you tell me about Narcan?" It was a question that haunted her, one that would forever remain unanswered.

According to Rebecca, the sheriff's office has changed its policies since that tragic event in her life. Nothing can bring Caleb and Kyler back. Rebecca knew that. But she couldn't help but wonder if the outcome would've been different if she had information about Fentanyl and Narcan.

"If I knew then what I know now, I would have done things differently," Rebecca said.

Rebecca has made it her mission to tell every parent, teen, and school administrator she has access to about the dangers of fentanyl and other drugs. She vowed to get lawmakers to hear her story and that of tens of thousands of parents like her. According to the Centers for Disease Control and Prevention, fentanyl poisoning is the number one cause of death among people between the ages of eighteen and forty-five. More than 100,000 people died in 2023 from fentanyl poisoning.

"I don't want their deaths to be completely in vain," she said with conviction. "They were casualties of a war—a war China and the cartels are waging against us. I feel a responsibility to shed light on that." It was her way of making sense of the tragedy, determined to turn her pain into purpose and raise awareness about the battle being fought right in their own communities.

In March of 2023, Rebecca testified before members of Congress to share her story and how her son died.

Excerpt from Rebecca's testimony before Congress.

The year Caleb was born – 2000, there were approximately 20,000 drug-related deaths in the U.S. The year they died – 2020, there were over 100,000. And according to the CDC, "in 2021, 106,699 drug overdose deaths occurred." The problem I have with that statement, that phrase "drug overdose", is that my 2 sons didn't die from overdosing on the drug they thought they had. They didn't die from an overdose of Percocet. "A drug overdose is taking too much of a substance, whether it's prescription, over the counter, legal, or illegal." As with most drug deaths now, my sons died from fentanyl poisoning, which is an extremely important distinction.

Law enforcement made it clear to me that this fentanyl came from Mexico. You talk about children being taken away from their parents - my children were taken away from me.

I didn't know that people were dying - I didn't know that my boys were taking anything that could kill them - they didn't think that they were either. This is a war - act like it - do something.

- Rebecca Kiessling

Rebecca believes her sons want justice and are in heaven helping with this mission. She doesn't see her fight as merely being against the individual drug dealer who sold the lethal pill. To her, it's about the entire system—the border policies, the way dangerous substances are smuggled into communities, and the people behind it all. It's not just about holding one person accountable. It's about dismantling the structure allowing these tragedies to happen.

"There's so much involved in getting justice," she reflects, "and I truly believe my sons would want me to fight for this."

For Rebecca, it's not just a personal mission but a responsibility she feels deeply—a duty to see this through and protect others from the same devastating loss.

"I would have wanted someone to have warned me, Rebecca said. "The government's number one role is to protect our people, and they failed. My sons deserved to be protected. I didn't know what fentanyl was, but our government knew."

While every school has its own anti-drug campaign, Rebecca says more needs to be done. That involves educating kids about the dangers of substance abuse starting at a young age.

Rebecca believes preventing tragedies like the one that took her sons' lives requires more than the occasional visit from a sheriff warning kids to stay away from drugs. That, she insists, simply isn't enough. She envisions a more profound, lasting impact—one where schools mandate that students hear testimony from families who have lost loved ones to drugs.

"They need to hear the stories from parents and siblings who have lived through it," she emphasizes. For Rebecca, these real-life experiences are what can truly resonate with young people making the danger personal and unforgettable

In addition, Rebecca wants every school district and law enforcement agency to have resources available on their websites for parents and addicted people who need help. She says it won't cost anything because the DEA already has all the information.

Rebecca is also working to change how cause of death is determined. She wants to see truth in autopsy reports. She has discovered a disturbing reality while advocating for justice after her sons' deaths. In many municipalities, there is no investigation into the true cause of death. No autopsies are being performed and grieving parents are often left with a death certificate listing suicide or accident as the cause when, in fact, it was homicide.

The system wasn't just failing her family—it was failing countless others. "These poor parents are being denied the truth and no one is even investigating."

Another procedural change Rebecca is pushing for is to require toxicology reports if there is a mysterious death. She said a lot of municipalities don't want homicides documented because it raises statistics on violent crime.

It's been four years since Rebecca lost her two sons, Caleb and Kyler. There isn't a moment she doesn't think about them. Time doesn't make things easier. Rebecca says there are moments when she thrives but mainly focuses on surviving. Her family and faith help her through the excruciating pain.

Rebecca realized that in order to cope, she had to find balance. "I have to pace myself, redirect and do things that bring me joy, like biking and performing stand-up comedy." It was her way of healing, of finding moments of light in the midst of darkness. She often reflects on the wisdom of the Bible, which says there's a time for both laughter and tears. "We can't always live in grief and expect to thrive and survive," she reminded herself. It was a lesson she carried with her. Rebecca finds joy in small things as she navigates her pain.

Kyler graduated high school the day before he died. The day after their deaths, Rebecca found a paper on which Kyler wrote out these goals just weeks before:

1. Stay away from drugs and alcohol. It's not worth it.
2. Surround myself with people who are well influenced.
3. Stay away from nicotine.
4. Treat people with more respect. Don't burn bridges.
5. Find another method to cope that works for me.
6. Get closer with Jaden (his girlfriend.)
7. Start doing something physical to get in shape.
8. Start working a lot to stay focused.
9. Finish school!!
10. Have a better relationship with my parents.
11. Do anything and everything to better myself and my health.

12. Listen when told to do something.
13. Don't f--- up or I'll have a felony on my record!!
14. Report to any and every drug test.
15. Don't follow in my birth mom's footsteps. (He loved her dearly, though ♥)
16. Be there for my brother, my only blood brother.
17. I can do anything I put my mind and effort into. Learn from this experience and never come back. This is not the lifestyle I want."-Kyler Kiessling

Rebecca is a wounded healer. She is a mom, activist, lawyer, and woman determined to spread her message and make changes in this country so no other parent will have to endure what she did.

Not only is Rebecca making an impact, but the legacy of Caleb and Kyler are also. One of Rebecca's son's friends told her that he stopped doing drugs completely after her boys died.

He approached her with a somber expression wanting to share something weighing on his mind. "I want you to know," he began, "that your boy's death sparked a movement in our area. It's now taboo to bring pills around."

His words struck her deeply. Though nothing could ease the pain of her loss, knowing that her sons' deaths led to change making others more cautious, brought her a small measure of comfort.

For Rebecca, it's a journey of taking things one day at a time. Through her mission and by sharing her story, she hopes to make a difference and save lives along the way.

"If you're a child of God, you do not just 'go around once' on Earth. You don't get just one earthly life. You get another one that is far better and without end. You'll inhabit the New Earth! You'll live with the God you cherish and the people you love as an undying person on an undying Earth."

— Randy Alcorn, Heaven

Resources:

- https://rebeccakiessling.com/
- Substance Abuse and Mental Health Services Administration (SAMHSA)-www.samhsa.gov
- National Institute on Drug Abuse (NIDA) - www.drugabuse.gov
- Narcotics Anonymous (NA)- www.na.org
- Al-Anon/Alateen - www.al-anon.org
- FindTreatment.gov-www.findtreatment.gov

Amy Singleton

Chapter 4
You are Not Too Much

"If you are broken, you do not have to stay broken."

-Selena Gomez

These words echo the depths of despair Amy Singleton faced—a woman who had long been told she was "too much" and "too loud." With childhood dreams of the stage, she often claimed Dolly Parton and Kenny Rogers were her true parents.

"I knew I was born for the stage. I was going to be an actor, dancer, or singer but there was a problem," she recalled.

Growing up, Amy struggled with her weight. She viewed herself as chubby and awkward. In her quest to fit in, she joined the drama and debate club and even became her high school's mascot. After graduation, she married her childhood sweetheart whom she met at twelve. The world seemed to open for her. She no longer had to worry about fitting in with the cool kids.

Ambitious and determined, Amy pursued a nursing degree but her genuine desire was to become a doctor. Yet fear held her back and she shifted her goals and dreams once again. "I let fear, my unhealthy relationship with money, and negative mindset affect some of my goals and aspirations when I was younger," she admitted.

As a dedicated operating room nurse and mother of two boys, Amy faced the challenges of a demanding career. Nursing is anything but a nine-to-five job—it's a high-stress environment with twelve-hour shifts. Amid it all, Amy put everyone else first and struggled with her weight reaching at 285 pounds.

One casualty of this time in her life was her marriage. She and her childhood sweetheart divorced. "I loved him so much, but he was gay and we weren't meant to be forever. It was like I experienced a death in my life. My husband was gone. My identity was tied to him."

Amy hoped to regain control of her life after her divorce. Long before the split, she had scheduled gastric bypass surgery believing it would improve her health her entire existence.

Amy started dating again and found someone she clicked with—the second love of her life. He was an avid outdoorsman. Since her weight loss surgery and renewed physique, she was able to do things she couldn't when she was obese.

She enjoyed the freedom her healthy body provided. One beautiful day, Amy rode her boyfriend's four-wheeler, rolled it over, and broke her back.

Her broken back was just the beginning. Shortly after the accident, Amy had a miscarriage and was diagnosed with cervical cancer which led to a total hysterectomy. During that time, Amy says her health took a nosedive.

Amy remembered the uncertainty and fear that filled those days. The doctors couldn't figure out what was happening to her. Her white blood cell count dropped to zero, baffling them. They suspected leukemia but couldn't be sure. The waiting and wondering felt endless, with no clear answers in sight.

After dozens of tests and doctors' appointments, Amy was told she had rheumatoid arthritis, lupus, and a whole host of other autoimmune disorders. With all her health issues she could no longer work. To add to the heartbreak, she and her boyfriend broke up. Amy was alone.

The once independent, working mom of two was wheelchair bound living at home with her parents. Pain was a constant companion. She required thirty-five different medications for everything from the pain to the mental anguish. Amy's agony was so unbearable the doctor prescribed methadone due to a growing tolerance to the narcotics.

You name it, she was on it.

The physical toll is only part of the story. The medications wreaked havoc on her mental health.

"I had a mental breakdown," Amy recalled. "With steroids and all the interactions, I was hearing voices and having visual and auditory hallucinations."

The dysfunction became so debilitating she was admitted to a mental health facility under lockdown.

Upon her release, Amy made a pivotal decision. Using her nursing expertise, she recognized the mountain of medications was obstructing her healing. "If I wanted my life back, I had to get off them as soon as possible," Amy stated.

Taking matters into her own hands, Amy gradually weaned herself off the medications—something she urges others not to attempt without a doctor's supervision.

Do not stop medications without a doctor's supervision.

Once she was finally free of her chemical life, Amy was still hurting physically and emotionally.

Not knowing where else to turn for relief, Amy sought alcohol to help manage the pain. Reflecting upon this experience, she admits she should have seen the red flags.

Alcoholism wasn't new to her family. Her grandfather & uncle imbibed. Statistically, those who have had gastric bypass surgery are also at higher risk of addiction. "I was in a terrible place," Amy admitted. "Whenever my boys went back to their dad's house, I binged for days. I was so depressed I completely disconnected from everyone around me." The pain in her voice was unmistakable as she described the isolation and struggle she faced during that difficult time.

Amy reached a point where she couldn't eat, bathe, or turn on the TV. She had bed sores because she couldn't leave her couch to make a sandwich or clean a dish.

She remembered the crushing hopelessness consuming her. There were moments when she believed the world would be better off without her. She even believed her boys would be better off without her.

Time after time, she found herself holding a handful of pills, the weight of it all pressing down on her. She was tempted to swallow them. Ending it all seemed the only viable answer. The darkness felt inescapable, those heavy moments lingered like a shadow over her memory.

Yet, in this darkness, Amy says she knew Jesus was right by her side and she had turned her back on Him.

The Lord works in mysterious ways.

One day, after feeling a slight shift toward healing, Amy opened Facebook to post something—a step she hadn't taken in a while. She received a call from a friend who saw the post and insisted on visiting her for lunch. "He said I was better than this. What happened to me sucked, but I needed to put one foot in front of the other," Amy recalled.

It was a turning point. Little by little, Amy rose from her couch—one step to brush her hair, another to make toast, and then collect the mail that had piled up. She reconnected with her community and even explored dating apps.

Again, Jesus works in mysterious ways.

Amy met a man on an app called Plenty of Fish. This gentleman had run in the same circles as her for decades prior, but they'd never connected until the perfect moment. Amy and Joseph dated long distances and eventually fell in love. Amy says he helped her see her value in herself. As of this writing, they celebrate six years of marriage and sobriety together.

Life was finally coming together for Amy and her husband. She was physically and mentally feeling better and surrounded by love and children.

Amy's condition prevented her return to nursing. Joseph still lived out of state early in the marriage, running his own business. As they thought about ways to serve their community, Joseph recalled the terrible experiences he had with "marketers & website people" in the past. What if they started a marketing agency? "Businesses deserve a relationship with a marketing firm they can trust." Joseph said. He was a serial entrepreneur. Amy was born to lead, communicate and help people. A new business model was born.

Amy and Joseph's enjoyment of what they did impressed clients. They experienced huge success—so much so that they partnered with Hite Digital. Amy and her team now serve 600 clients coast to coast for digital marketing needs and have reached the Inc. 5000 list three years in a row.

Amy's journey wasn't just about career success. The girl who once dreamed of the stage is now an emcee, speaker, and the host of a top 10% podcast called Queens Lead. However, overcoming self-doubt is an ongoing process. "Loving myself and reconnecting with that young girl," Amy reflected, "has been part of the healing. I'm conversing with young Amy, telling her she was okay all along."

It's been a journey of self-acceptance, learning to embrace the person she once was and still is.

Amy has been able to heal through therapy and mindset coaching. Not only mentally but physically, as she continues to deal with rheumatoid arthritis. Amy says she had to heal herself from the inside out. This started with mindset work.

Amy enlisted the help of mindset coach Jose Bolanos. His program teaches about the polarities of life, which are the ups and downs of life. In Amy's case, it was health's ups and downs. Before ice baths were trendy, Amy took plunges in cold water and used the sauna to help her body. She learned intentionally stressing your body's upper or lower limits can help you be steadier when those upper and lower limits are pressed. Without fail, life will press all the limits.

"The bottom is going to drop out at some point," Amy said. "Your partner might leave, someone close to you could die, or you'll face a difficult diagnosis." She paused, her voice steady with determination. "But the more you can prepare your body and mind to handle hard things, the better. I remind myself constantly—I can do hard things. I was made for this." It's a mantra she lives by—a source of strength when life feels overwhelming.

Healing is a journey, not a destination. Through prayer, meditation, healthy eating, and exercise Amy cherishes the support she has received along the way.

Recently, Amy was baptized again to express her reconnected faith and love for God. She says she has never felt so close to Jesus and couldn't do anything without him.

If Amy could speak to her ten-year-old self, she would say: "You are not too much. Not everyone is going to like you, and that's okay. When you find the people who share your values and interests, the ones who support you, those against you won't matter. Seek Jesus for yourself and know who He is—not what a preacher says. Seek for yourself and find that relationship."

Amy's story is one of resilience, transformation, and the power of self-love—a testament to the strength of the human spirit.

Resources

- The Big Leap
- Supercommunicators
- The Mel Robbins Podcast.
- Bible Project.
- AmySingleton.Com
- https://www.hitedigital.com/norman
- https://queenslead.org/

Chapter 5
37 Days in Jail

"Prison might have stripped me down, but I rebuilt my life out of those ashes."

-Susan Burton

In this chapter, we have chosen to keep this brave woman's name anonymous to protect her privacy and well-being. Given the highly sensitive nature of her situation and the potential risks that public exposure could pose to her and her family, maintaining her anonymity is critical. Sharing her real identity could invite unwanted attention, legal complications, and even threats to her safety. For this book she is going by the name Sarah. By preserving her privacy, we allow Sarah to tell her story and impart the lessons she's learned without jeopardizing her personal security or the welfare of those she loves.

Sarah had always believed she was living the American dream. She had carved out a successful career in the television industry, all while raising three children. Her hard work and dedication earned her prestigious awards and recognition from the president of the United States. On the surface, it seemed like Sarah had it all.

But life can change in an instant, and for Sarah, that moment came unexpectedly. She went from being a respected professional and devoted mother to facing the unthinkable; time in prison, her future uncertain, and her safety at constant risk. The woman who had once stood in the spotlight now found herself in the darkest of shadows, fearful of what might come next.

"I believe I was punished for standing up for myself," said Sarah. "And for not being afraid as a female in an area where it's all male driven. I didn't stand a chance."

Sarah had been battling a divorce case for thirteen years in family court. However, in 2016, the family court turned into a criminal court. And her life changed forever.

As part of her divorce agreement, Sarah was required to sell the house she and her ex-husband owned. Before it could go on the market, the court ordered her to make necessary repairs, including fixing damage caused by a leak. Thankfully, insurance was set to cover some of the costs.

But that's when things took an unexpected turn. Her ex-husband accused her of forging his signature on a check from the insurance company. In response, the judge ordered all their joint checking accounts to be closed, adding even more stress to an already difficult situation.

Shortly after that, she received a call from the police. They told her she was going to be arrested unless she turned herself in. Sarah went to the police station and was charged with petty larceny, fingerprinted, and arraigned for forgery.

She recalled the day with clarity, determined to set the record straight. "I didn't forge his name," she explained. The check had been made out to both of them, and when she took it to the bank, she signed her own name. The teller had asked if the other signature was his, and she had been honest. "No, that's my signature," she had said. The bank president at that branch had stepped in, reassuring her. "We're going to open an account for you," he said. "Can you just print your name underneath so we know it's you?" She agreed without hesitation, doing everything in plain sight. "It was all on camera at the bank," she added, emphasizing her transparency in the situation.

Sarah says by law the check had to stay in the account for eight days. After the eight days she took the money out and paid the hired person to fix the house.

After getting arrested, Sarah knew this story would be on the news. This was awkward because she was a journalist—a public figure in that local news market. To minimize her humiliation, she urged her attorneys to hold a press conference so her side would be told. But her attorneys didn't think the story was newsworthy.

Just as Sarah had predicted, at exactly five o'clock, the news broke across all local media outlets. The television station where she had worked for years received the press release right away, and soon enough, her mugshot was plastered on screens throughout the market where she built her career. Sarah says that no one reached out to hear her side of the story. By the time she even had a chance to explain, she had already lost her job,

Jobless and fighting to escape jail, Sarah did everything she could to clear her name and protect her kids. It was taking a toll on her family.

She had always been a law-abiding citizen, never in trouble with the law. But during that difficult period, everything seemed to fall apart for her and her kids. "It was devastating," she recalled. The stress felt like it was tearing her body apart. She underwent three biopsies during that time and even started blacking out from the overwhelming strain. "It was just horrible," she said, the memory of that painful chapter still vivid.

A few weeks prior, Sarah was presenting stories on the news. Now her mugshot was being plastered all over the news shows, blogs, and social media.

Throughout the process, Sarah documented everything trying to prove the court system made numerous mistakes. She wrote about it in detail in her book, which will be released next year.

The petty larceny charges were dropped, but Sarah was then charged with possessing a forged instrument. Sarah alleges the charges are bogus.

Sarah said there is no proof the check was forged. "He didn't sign it, so how could it have been forgery?", she questioned.

The case went to trial. When she left the house, Sarah kissed her three kids goodbye not knowing if she would return.

"Every day, I would get dressed, and I didn't know if I would be found guilty or if they would let me go home, Sarah recalled. "Was I going to be coming back to my family?"

Sarah's attorneys told her not to worry about anything and that she wasn't going to jail. She was told the worst-case scenario is that she will have to do community service.

The trial lasted three days. The jury had reached a verdict. Sarah stood quietly shaking as she waited.

The verdict?

Guilty.

As Sarah stood in the courtroom, she glanced at each member of the jury, disbelief washing over her. The verdict had come, and the judge wasted no time—she was immediately sentenced to jail. The shock on her attorney's face was unforgettable. He pleaded with the judge, reminding him that Sarah had three children waiting for her at home and she never committed a crime. But the judge was unmoved. Without hesitation, the judge ordered her to jail.

The judge looked at her sternly and asked, "Do you understand the charges? You could face up to eight years in federal prison. Do you understand this?"

She nodded and replied, "I do, Your Honor, but I didn't do anything wrong." Despite the gravity of the situation, she remained resolute, determined to stand by her innocence.

As the officers approached, they asked Sarah if she was okay. She nodded and reassured them, "I'm fine. I'm good." Sitting there in silence, something unexpected happened—a profound sense of peace washed over her. It wasn't fear or panic, but a calm acceptance. In that moment, Sarah realized she didn't know how she would get out of this or what the future held, but she was at peace with herself. She knew, deep down, she had done nothing wrong.

Sarah was handcuffed and brought in the police car as they took the ten-minute ride to jail. The peace turned into panic, and she cried uncontrollably. She arrived and had to strip herself of everything. Jewelry, clothes, shoes. Her mind spun out of control.

"Who's going to get me out?" She exclaimed. "Oh my God, am I going to be here forever? The judge said eight years, so I started doing the math, and my kids will be 21. I will miss my whole life, my kids' entire life."

As she walked down the corridor, dressed in green pants and a green shirt, holding a towel and toothbrush, she heard the doors shut behind her. Reality set in. The only assuring words she heard were from a female officer saying, "Don't worry, you'll be okay."

Sitting in a twelve foot by four cell, Sarah waited for attorney to get her out.

He never came.

Sarah still had her one phone call but couldn't remember anyone's number. Wracking her brain, she called her friend and explained everything. Her friend and a cousin came to see her right away.

She remembered the moment vividly, the helplessness overwhelming her. She couldn't even hug her children because there was a barrier of plastic between them. Desperation crept in as she turned to her cousin, her voice trembling. She told them to "get her out of there." The weight of the situation sank deeper with every passing minute.

But Sarah wasn't getting out that weekend because it was Memorial Day. The courts were closed. Once the weekend passed, she hoped she would get out.

Sarah spent thirteen long days in that twelve-by-four cell using much of her time to pray. On the thirteenth day, she felt her prayers had been answered. A new attorney, who had heard about her case stepped in and quickly filed for a bail hearing. As she prepared to face the court once more, Sarah clung to the hope that this would be the last time she would ever see that cold, confining cell again.

She walked into the Supreme Court with her hands and feet chained and stood before the judge. Bail was granted. Sarah was free to go home for now, but she still had to face sentencing.

On probation, Sarah was finally able to hug her children again.

Throughout the divorce case and legal fees to defend herself, Sarah says she spent close to $600,000. Finances got so bad that she couldn't afford food or toilet paper and declared bankruptcy.

The day Sarah had been dreading was here.

Sentencing day.

She arrived at the courthouse not knowing when she would see her children again.

"I'll never forget my youngest daughter's face of panic," she recalled. "I hugged them, and I said, I love you."

Sarah was sentenced to four months in jail with credit for time served and five years of probation.

At her sentencing, Sarah disregarded her attorney's advice. She addressed the judge wanting him to hear her side. She was glad she spoke up. Sarah says that saved her because otherwise the judge would have sentenced her to six months or more.

Before heading to court that day, Sarah prepared herself for the worst. She had written down all the important phone numbers—her attorney's, her kids', her doctor's, and her family's—scribbled across her arms in case the anxiety overtook her. It had before, making her forgetful. She didn't bring any jewelry with her, knowing she wouldn't want to leave anything valuable behind if things took a turn. Every small detail was planned, as she braced herself for what might come next.

Handcuffed again, placed in the police car, and making that familiar trip to the jail, Sarah tried to come to grips with the fact that for the next four months, this was going to be her life.

To survive, Sarah trained her mind to think she was living her prison life as a different person. She also turned to her faith.

In the early days of her time in jail, Sarah asked the officer for a pen, paper, and some books. She soon found herself in the jail's small library where the first book that caught her eye was the Bible. In that moment, she felt a quiet reassurance wash over her. Despite being physically alone, she realized she wasn't truly by herself—God was with her. Determined not to lose her faith, Sarah made a promise to hold on to it, spending her time reading the Bible, particularly finding solace in the book of John.

Sarah also discovered she was good at playing ping-pong. Other inmates dubbed her the ping-pong queen. While doing everything she could to forget she was stuck there for four months, Sarah began doing what she was best at—interviewing other inmates and writing their stories which gave her an outlet.

Thirty-seven days into jail time, Sarah heard from her attorneys that they were going to the appellate court to try to get her sentence cut. Later that day, Sarah got the news she had been praying for. When the appellate court reviewed her case, they concluded the judge had abused his power. They declared the time Sarah had already served was sufficient. In that moment, a wave of relief washed over her—she was finally getting out. She would soon be going home to see her children.

On that final day in jail, Sarah walked down the same cold corridor she entered. She no longer wore the green pants and shirt. Sporting her old clothes and cheers from some of her friends made while in prison echoed off the walls. Could this be real? Finally, Sarah was going to hug her children again.

Life was far from easy as Sarah re-entered her role as mother. She was broke. Her reputation was ruined. The company she worked for had gone out of business. Knowing she had to provide, Sarah took the only job she could find cleaning kitchens and bathrooms. She made ten dollars an hour while paying her babysitter fifteen. Hard to believe she was once a successful journalist.

Sarah's legal battles surrounding her divorce continued for years after her release from jail. Time behind bars changes a person. Sarah found she had to reinvent herself. She said spending time behind bars taught her street smarts, how the legal system worked, and how precious life is.

Sarah started a successful cleaning business and focused on rebuilding her life. Part of that journey was writing a book about her ordeal through family and criminal court and her life in prison. The book also includes stories of the women she interviewed while incarcerated.

"I've met a lot of women in jail, and some of them didn't make it—they committed suicide," she shared, her voice filled with sadness. "I want others to understand that no matter how hard it gets, you can overcome." Reflecting on her own time in jail, she explained, "I refused to be depressed, no matter what was happening around me. I was defeated, exhausted, and cried until I couldn't cry anymore. I never let myself sink into depression." Even after getting out, when she was struggling to pay bills and life felt overwhelming, she found a way to push through. "I would shower, get dressed, put on my makeup, and wear my high heels," she said with a quiet strength. "I found that power within me."

Nothing can take back the years Sarah spent in court or the weeks that she was in jail. Nothing can bring back the money she spent on legal fees. Nothing can be done to erase the news articles with her mugshot. But she is okay with that. Sarah is stronger, smarter, and more resilient than ever.

Sarah has a new life with her family, a new career, a new book, and a new outlook on life.

Sarah reflected on her journey, her voice filled with pride. "Everything I've been through has made me who I am today," she said with conviction. A smile crossed her face as she added, "And I am so proud of who I am today." It was clear that the challenges she had faced had only strengthened her, shaping her into the person she had become.

Resources

- The Bible

Scarlett Lewis

Jesse Lewis

Chapter 6
Choose Love

"A mother never truly loses a child. She carries them with her forever, in her heart, her memories, and her very being."

-Katherine Jackson

It was a cold December morning, just two weeks before Christmas. Scarlett Lewis, a single mother, was busy getting her two sons, JT and Jesse, ready for school. JT, her seventh grader, was preparing to head out to the Newtown, Connecticut Middle School. Jesse, just six years old, was excited about his mom coming to his first-grade class at Sandy Hook Elementary School later to help make gingerbread houses. The morning routine carried a sense of warmth and quiet excitement as the holiday season drew near.

Jesse's dad was in the driveway, ready to take his son to school. Scarlett went outside to say goodbye to Jesse. She turned to hug him and saw he'd written 'I LOVE YOU' in the frost on the car door. Scarlett wanted to capture that moment, so she ran into the house to get her phone and take a picture.

"I remember gently guiding him by the shoulder, bundled up in his little winter coat, and positioning him by the car so I could capture him and his message in the same frame," Scarlett recalled. "I took the picture, but it was overexposed because of the morning sun, so I took another one and then a close-up of his message, 'I LOVE YOU.' Afterward, I hugged him and sent him off with his dad."

Later that morning, while at work, rumors about a shooting in Sandy Hook swirled around the office. It never crossed Scarlett's mind it could be at Jesse's elementary school.

Scarlett vividly remembered when someone approached her and asked, "Doesn't your son go to Sandy Hook Elementary School?" Panic immediately set in. Without hesitation, she entered her car and began the forty-five-minute drive to the school. As she neared the campus, her heart sank. Helicopters were circling overhead, and emergency vehicles flooded the area. The scene before her confirmed her worst fears, and overwhelming dread consumed her as she approached the chaos.

Pulse-pounding, Scarlett bolted from her car and tried to talk to anyone who could give her information.

It was chaos.

Next, she decided to head to the firehouse, where evacuated children were held, but Jesse wasn't there. Where was Jesse? A witness reported the boy may have gone to a neighboring house.

But he wasn't there.

The homeowner told Scarlett to check at the daycare.

But he wasn't there.

Panic flaring, Scarlett instructed Jesse's father to search at the hospital while she continued her search of the neighborhood around the school.

She tried to enter the school, but they wouldn't let her in. Scarlett found it alarming they wouldn't let a mother searching for her child into the building. Law Enforcement instructed her to add Jesse's name to a missing child list. Still, the reality of the situation wasn't resolving in her mind.

As Scarlett approached the list of missing children, her heart sank. When it came time to write Jesse's name, the front of the page was already filled. With trembling hands, she turned the sheet over and wrote his name on the back. The weight of the growing list of names pressed heavily on her chest.

The families of the missing children stood in agonizing uncertainty outside Sandy Hook Elementary huddled together in the biting December cold. Hours passed like days as they clung to any sliver of hope, desperate for news. Every minute felt unbearable as the silence from inside the school stretched on. They scanned every face that emerged, hoping to see their child walk out unharmed. But no one knew—no one could say where their children were or if they were alive or gone forever. The air was thick with fear and despair as the reality of the tragedy began to sink in. The unspoken dread lingered between them.

The parents didn't know at the time, but as they waited for answers inside the Sandy Hook fire house, the officials were busy counting and trying to identify the bodies.

Jesse's older brother, JT, arrived from the middle school to wait with his mom for news of Jesse's whereabouts. The uncertainty loomed heavily in the air, as no one knew whether the threat had spread to other schools. Parents had been anxiously clutching their phones listening for updates while teachers tried to maintain calm amidst rising fear. There was a brief moment of relief when JT arrived, but it was quickly overshadowed by the dread that Jesse was still unaccounted for. The police were working tirelessly, but chaos reigned as families and school officials scrambled for information unsure if more danger was lurking nearby. Every passing moment without answers deepened the sense of helplessness and fear that something unspeakable had happened. This reality became more challenging to ignore.

Authorities peppered the families with questions to help with identification. The officers were trying to maintain a sense of calm as they spoke to Scarlett, but their questions made the gravity of the situation undeniable. They gently asked if she had a recent picture of Jesse, and if there were any identifying marks on his body. Her mind raced, trying to recall anything that might help. Then she remembered.

Jesse had a small mole on his right foot. Clinging to that detail, she gave them the information, her voice trembling as the surreal weight of the moment pressed down on her.

As the day wore on, hope faded. Police told the families that their children were killed in the shooting. Scarlett's son, Jesse, was one of them.

By that point, Scarlett's family was by her side. There was nothing more they could do at the school. A van returned the family to their cars. Scarlett remembers looking in her car with her mom as a horrifying realization hit her.

Her eyes landed on the backseat. There it was—Jesse's car seat, a reminder of his smallness and innocence. He was only six years old—still using it for every ride. A painful realization washed over her. I won't need that car seat anymore, she thought, her heart breaking as the weight of what had happened settled in.

Scarlett didn't know what to do or think. She was a mom who just found out her six-year-old had been murdered. The emotions were endless, and the thought of returning home where Jesse had eaten breakfast just hours before was unfathomable.

While trying to be strong for Jesse's brother, JT, Scarlett tried to remain stoic.

"I couldn't imagine returning to my farmhouse," Scarlett thought. "In my mind, it was like walking through the door and seeing Jesse's boots. Going into the bathroom, I saw his toothbrush. Going into the bedroom, I saw his PJs and where he had left them. I was never going to go back. I was never going to step foot in that house again."

Scarlett and her son JT stayed with friends and family, surrounded by people who could support her in the darkest moments.

Scarlett's focus was survival and the mental health of Jesse's older brother, JT. Finding time to grieve and process what had happened was extremely difficult. Scarlett said the reality of what happened set in when she had time alone. Her body was in shock.

"Your body takes over and helps you walk and do things you must do," Scarlett recalled. "I looked at my face in pictures from then and saw a vacancy in my eyes. I remember the pain being so excruciating. I thought that I was going to dissolve. I was going to cease to exist as a human. Yet, I couldn't believe my body was continuing to live."

Scarlett didn't want to return to her house but knew she had to gather Jesse's clothes for his funeral. She wanted to be the one to dress Jesse in his casket, something she never imagined she would have to do—something a parent should never have to do.

Scarlett's return to her home was a heartbreaking ordeal. Her sister-in-law rented a van and the family drove back together. Scarlett remembers the heaviness in the air as she entered the house unable to face the memories around her. "I don't want to look at anything," she thought, determined to focus on one task: picking out clothes for Jesse.

With single-minded purpose, she headed straight for Jesse's room. As she stood in front of his dresser, practical thoughts began to surface through her grief. It was cold outside, and she wanted Jesse to be warm. She carefully selected flannel-lined jeans, a turtleneck, one of his favorite gray pullovers, warm socks, and boots. The boots felt particularly important—Jesse always wore boots on their farm. Each item of clothing held a connection to the child she had lost, and yet, in this devastating moment, they also became symbols of her final act of motherly care. Once she had completed the task, Scarlett knew she couldn't stay any longer.

After Scarlett gathered Jesse's clothes, she bolted from the house as quickly as possible, trying not to look at anything. Holding his clothes in her arms and laser-focused on the back door, something grabbed her attention.

She glanced over at the spray-painted chalkboard on the side of her oven and froze. There, written in Jesse's small handwriting, were the words 'Nurturing Healing Love.' These words were phonetically spelled, "Norturing Helinn Love," as he was in first grade and just learning to write. He had written them sometime shortly before he was killed. Her jaw dropped, and she stood in disbelief, staring at the message left behind. "We couldn't believe it," she said, overwhelmed by the significance of those words as if they were a final gift from him.

Then, Scarlett pondered the message six-year-old Jesse left—a message she didn't know was there until that moment.

As the media, parents, and the community buzzed with discussions about school safety and gun violence, she couldn't shake a different thought. Everyone was searching for solutions, but the answer was clear to her. No, she thought, this is the solution. The words "nurturing, healing, love" echoed in her mind. "That's what Adam Lanza was missing," she realized. "Love feels good, and anger, hatred, and resentment—those feed bad." She believed that if Adam had been able to feel good about himself honestly, he would never have wanted to hurt others.

Adam Lanza was the gunman who killed twenty-first graders and six school employees before turning a gun on himself. Earlier that day, he killed his mother at the home they shared. Scarlett learned from the state police that Jesse had saved nine of his first-grade classmates before his life was taken. Jesse, showing incredible bravery, yelled for his classmates to run. His actions allowed several of them to escape the room before the gunman could take more lives. In her grief, knowing that Jesse had acted selflessly in his final moments, gave Scarlett a sense of pride and solace knowing her son made a difference.

"These words that Jesse wrote changed my mind set and I realized spreading this message was my purpose," Scarlett exclaimed.

Scarlett, a single working mom, assumed she was returning to work but says that after she saw Jesse's words on the chalkboard about nurturing, healing, and love, she knew her calling had changed. Scarlett was not going back to work. She was going to follow her heart and Jesse's words.

"I had to ensure our kids were safe," Scarlett insisted. "What happened to Jesse was preventable. And I knew I had to make sure this doesn't happen to other kids because this didn't have to happen to Jesse."

Scarlett found herself grappling with the overwhelming question: What is the root cause of school shootings? She realized the issue went beyond gun control or security measures; it was about emotional and social health. Scarlett sought something deeper that connected all humans—a fundamental need to love and be loved.

While wrestling with her grief and searching for answers, Scarlett envisioned a movement that could unite people across political, social, and ideological divides. She wanted to focus on universal human needs which transcended tragedy and could unite communities. In January 2013, the Choose Love Movement was born. The initiative aimed at addressing the emotional intelligence and compassion that could prevent future violence became Scarlett's mission.

Scarlett wanted to amplify "Nurturing Healing Love" in schools but needed help. She visited a doctoral professor to learn more about social-emotional learning. Scarlett had never heard of Social and Emotional Learning (SEL) before Jesse's death, but when she came across it, she instantly recognized its importance. After researching, she realized how critical these skills were, not just for herself but for everyone. SEL equips people with the tools to navigate life's challenges, and she understood that these essential life skills were vital to flourishing in the face of adversity. Scarlett felt deeply that if children were taught these principles—courage, forgiveness, gratitude, and compassion—it could change lives.

As she dug deeper into SEL, she saw that it was all backed by evidence-based research, validating its effectiveness. She became convinced that every child should have access to these tools. In her heart, Scarlett knew these skills had the power to prevent tragedies like the one that claimed her son. If Adam Lanza had learned how to face his pain instead of letting it consume him, things could have turned out differently. She believed that SEL was about personal growth and stopping future violence by teaching people how to learn from, grow through, and be strengthened by their pain. This insight became the foundation for her mission through the Choose Love Movement, a way to honor Jesse's memory and ensure his death would not be in vain.

Scarlett created Jesse's formula by breaking down the definitions of "Nurturing Healing Love." Nurturing means loving, kindness, and gratitude. Healing means forgiveness. Love is compassion in action. The formula is simple: Courage, plus gratitude, plus forgiveness, plus compassion, and action, equal choosing love.

Scarlett learned that humans were created to be strengthened by life's challenges and pain. She found certain simple skills, tools and awarenesses, rooted in neuroscience provide a pathway to thriving. By taking responsibility, adding character, and the power of choice, kids and adults could be empowered to have healthy connections and feel a deep sense of belonging. When the locus of control is external—when individuals blame, point fingers, or fault others, they fall into a cycle of victimization. This often leads to a sense of hopelessness which tragically, is one of the critical indicators of violence and suicide.

The process she developed was designed to shift this locus of control inward, bringing power back within the individual. This internal shift builds self-esteem, increases self-confidence, and enhances one's belief in one's ability to influence what's happening in one's life. This is the definition of hope. Scarlett recognized that empowering people in this way could prevent the very cycle that leads to tragedies like the one at Sandy Hook.

Scarlett collaborated with multiple education and mental health professionals to create this program. The goal was to make it available to preschoolers and continue it until they graduated from high school.

Scarlett embraced copious amounts of research showing the earlier emotional intelligence and social-emotional learning were introduced, the better the outcomes for children. She started implementing these practices from prenatal, infant/toddler, and pre-kindergarten through fifth grade, understanding that brain development begins far earlier than most people realize. Reflecting on her own experiences as a mother, she wished she had known these insights sooner. If only new mothers understood the importance of infant brain development and the simple things they could do to optimize it. This awareness fueled her commitment to educate parents and children alike on the significance of emotional intelligence from an early age.

The program was an instant success. Scarlett eventually extended the Choose Love Movement through middle and high school and opened it to parents, foster care, government agencies, and corrections programs.

The comprehensive, year-long program is estimated to be in 14,500 schools and has received 100,000 downloads on their website, ChooseLoveMovement.org. It is also no-cost as Scarlett believes this program could have saved not only her son's life and the others, but his attacker's as well.

The Choose Love Movement has four pillars and teaches students how to respond with love in any situation using the Choose Love Formula:

Courage: The willingness to work through obstacles, even when feeling fear, embarrassment, or uncertainty.

Gratitude: Being thankful, even when things are challenging.

Forgiveness: Letting go of anger and resentment and moving forward.

Compassion-in-Action: Understanding the suffering of others and acting to help.

The response from parents, teachers, and students has been overwhelming. Scarlett says their encouragement keeps her going.

"I was speaking at a school in New Hampshire, and they've had such success that their attendance has significantly improved," Scarlett exclaimed. "Additionally, behavioral issues have drastically decreased. One student, who had previously refused to attend school, was introduced to the Choose Love program and now has 100% attendance. He's happier, healthier, and making friends—just like that!"

"Dear Scarlett, Thank you for the Choose Love Formula. Before it, I was hopeless and discouraged myself. But now I am encouraging people and myself. Thank you for all that you've done. You're getting me through all this stuff and days. I love you."

Scarlett says stories like that have made her realize over the last few years that this is our purpose on earth. I asked Scarlett if she had let go of her anger about Jesse's murder on that cold December day.

Scarlett told me she never felt anger toward Adam Lanza, even in the wake of the unimaginable tragedy. Instead, she found herself understanding that anyone capable of committing such a horrific act must have been in tremendous pain. In the following days, she witnessed blame cast in every direction—fingers pointing at individuals, systems, and institutions. But she couldn't help but think, No, that's too easy. "When do we start taking responsibility for what's happening in our communities?" she wondered. It wasn't about blame but understanding and addressing the deeper issues for her.

Scarlett took on the responsibility of helping these suffering children. She wanted to teach them the skills needed to cope with difficult situations.

She came to a powerful realization: by accepting her part of the responsibility, she could do something about it. Instead of feeling helpless, she felt empowered. "Taking responsibility gave me the ability to act," she reflected. Understanding that this ownership fueled her strength and determination to make a difference.

A student asked Scarlett that if Jesse hadn't died, would she still be doing this—helping children and teachers?

Scarlett told the student that she wouldn't have. After losing Jesse, Scarlett sat on her mom's couch, overwhelmed by mixed emotions, including an unexpected realization. At first, the weight of grief was all-consuming, but soon she noticed something else—an absence of fear. Reflecting on her life, Scarlett recognized how many of her past decisions had been made from fear: relationships, jobs, countless moments. That clarity brought a commitment to change. She vowed never to live in fear again and instead embraced Jesse's message on the chalkboard: to live a life filled with love. From that moment, she promised herself she would choose love, just as Jesse had encouraged.

While Jesse is not here on earth, Scarlett says he is helping her every day with the Choose Love Movement.

"He's my CEO," Scarlett said. "Jesse is running the show, recruiting people to help me." Time and time again, people would come to her, telling her they felt like they had been recruited, driven by a powerful calling to be part of the mission. Scarlett knew it was Jesse guiding them, bringing opportunities her way that she could never have accessed alone. "I feel like he's saying, 'Mom, you just show up, and I'll make sure everything happens.'" It gave her a sense of comfort, knowing that in some way Jesse was still with her leading.

While Scarlett's focus is spreading Jesse's message, she encourages parents to advocate for their children because if they don't, who will? Scarlett says there is an urgent need to address the declining confidence kids in America have in their ability to feel safe at school. She encourages parents to engage in direct conversations with school officials, ideally in front of their children, to foster transparency and accountability.

Scarlett says parents should call their children's schools and ask pointed questions: "What kind of hardening measures do you have in place? How do you address grievances that may lead to violence? Do you offer a comprehensive Life Skills Program?" She believes schools should be prepared to answer these inquiries confidently. Additionally, she stresses the importance of community involvement, asking, "Is there a place where I can go to see what these programs teach?" By encouraging such dialogues, Scarlett hopes to empower parents and restore faith in the safety measures provided by educational institutions. No parent should ever have to lose a child as Scarlett did.

She felt deeply convinced about her purpose, believing that she and Jesse were brought into this world to share a powerful message. "If Jesse could stand up to the shooter and save nine of his classmates' lives," she thought, "then I can certainly carry that message forward." With that in mind, she found the strength to show up in schools and communities, determined to talk about the values of courage, love, and hope that her son embodied, keeping his spirit alive through her work.

God bless these children and teachers.

Sandy Hook Elementary School Shooting Victims

December 14, 2012

Students:

    Charlotte Bacon, 6
    Daniel Barden, 7
    Olivia Engel, 6
    Josephine Gay, 7
    Ana Marquez-Greene, 6
    Dylan Hockley, 6
    Madeleine Hsu, 6
    Catherine Violet Hubbard, 6
    Chase Kowalski, 7
    Jesse Lewis, 6
    James Mattioli, 6
    Grace McDonnell, 7
    Emily Parker, 6
    Jack Pinto, 6
    Noah Pozner, 6
    Caroline Previdi, 6

Staff:
- Dawn Hochsprung (Principal)
- Mary Sherlach (School Psychologist)
- Victoria Soto (Teacher)
- Lauren Rousseau (Teacher)
- Anne Marie Murphy (Special Education Teacher)
- Rachel D'Avino (Teacher's Aide)

Resources

- www.chooslovemovement.org

Amberly Lago

Chapter 7
You are Worthy

"You gain strength, courage, and confidence by every experience in which you really stop to look fear in the face. You are able to say to yourself, 'I lived through this horror. I can take the next thing that comes along.'"

- Eleanor Roosevelt

Childhood should be a time of joy and innocence, where the most pressing tasks involve choosing games and imaginative adventures. Safety within the walls of one's home should be a given. However, for young Amberly Lago of a small Texas town, this reality didn't exist.

At just eight years old, Amberly says she was sexually abused by her stepfather. The abuse continued for years, and he threatened to kill her mother if she ever told anyone. The threat was constant, trapping her in a shadow of fear, far removed from the carefree childhood she deserved.

When Amberly was thirteen, she mustered the courage to confide in her biological father about the abuse. However, she demanded he remain silent for fear of retaliation from her stepfather.

Her father met her demands and kept silent. "I felt unworthy of being protected," she recalled. "I didn't feel worthy of being loved." Since then, she and her dad reflected upon that vow of silence at length. Why didn't he tell someone who could intervene?

Her dad told her he respected her wishes.

How did he not see through her cry for help?

A spark ignited within her as she realized the truth. If I'm going to get better and get through this, she thought, it's up to me. The realization hit her hard, but it was empowering. "I have to step up," she resolved. "I have to protect myself." From that moment on, she knew her strength and healing would come from within, and it was up to her to take control of her own journey.

The next time Amberly's stepfather entered her room, she decided enough was enough. Despite the odds stacked against her, Amberly summoned her strength, fighting back with determination and landing a powerful punch. After that encounter, her stepfather never laid a hand on her again marking a crucial shift in her fight for her own safety and autonomy.

That incident taught empowered Amberly to take charge of her circumstances. Amberly learned at an early age that if we want more for ourselves, we must be ready to take the necessary steps to achieve that transformation.

To distract herself from her home life, Amberly poured her energy into athletics. She found solace in dance, becoming the youngest member of a competitive dance team. She also excelled in track, setting a state record for the fastest mile run by a girl in Texas. These outlets made Amberly feel accomplished and important.

Tragically, Amberly's two brothers never learned how to cope with their home life. One of her brothers is on death row, and the other has been in and out of a drug rehab facility.

Amberly's life highlights the vital role of having healthy outlets in our lives. She says it's essential to focus on activities and experiences that bring joy and positivity, as they not only uplift our spirits but also motivate us to strive for improvement. For her, nurturing these positive influences is key to personal growth and well-being.

Fitness continued to play a big role in Amberly's adult life. Healthy, fit, and an entrepreneur, Amberly built a business from the ground up where she taught other trainers how to get certified and run a fitness business. She was a dancer and a recognized fitness coach helping others achieve their dreams.

In 2010, Amberly was living her dream in California with her husband and two children. She had everything she wanted. When Amberly was thirty-eight, she had an accident that turned her life upside down.

On a beautiful sunny day in May, Amberly rode her Harley down Ventura Boulevard. She was struck by an SUV. The force of the impact propelled her thirty feet down the street, shattering her right leg. The damage was so severe, amputation was a possibility.

Amberly spent months in the hospital enduring thirty-four surgeries. During this time, she was diagnosed with an incurable nerve disease known as Complex Regional Pain Syndrome (CRPS), often referred to as the "suicide disease" due to the excruciating pain it causes. This condition ranks among the highest on the pain scale, making her journey even more challenging.

"This can't be my life," Amberly remembers thinking. "I lost the career I had built. We had $2.9 million worth of medical expenses and a lien on our house."

Amberly was the main breadwinner and now her income was gone. She went from working out every day to being deformed from the hip down. Her entire leg was full of metal from her knee to her toes.

The physical and mental pain Amberly endured is indescribable. There were many times she lost hope and mentally went down a dark path.

Amberly recalls how, every three hours, the nurses would change the bandages on her leg to prevent infection, exposing the raw, inside layers of her injury. One day, as she stared at her leg, a memory surfaced—an infomercial she had seen of a beautiful woman running along the beach, husband and family happily following her. The contrast between that image and her own reality spiraled Amberly into despair. She was consumed by fear. What if they amputate my leg tomorrow? What if I can never work again? What if my husband doesn't love me anymore? What if I can't chase after my kids? These thoughts weighed heavily on her deepening her sense of vulnerability and uncertainty.

These dark thoughts weren't helping her heal. Amberly made the difficult choice to shift her focus toward getting better. Gratitude became her best medicine.

Amberly stood at a crossroads knowing she had a choice to make. I can go down that road of despair, or I can focus on what I have right in front of me, right now. Determined to choose hope, she picked up a small notebook and began writing, capturing her thoughts and feelings. That notebook became her lifeline. It is something she still holds onto today as a reminder of the moment she chose to move forward.

Amberly began writing down the names of people who gave her flowers, gifts, and food. She also made a note of every nurse who came in to help her.

Amberly says that when she began writing what she was thankful for, she started to feel better, causing a shift in her perspective. She realized how fortunate she was just to be alive. Though she couldn't go outside, she reminded herself of the blessings she still had—the view from her window and the clear blue sky. Filled with hope, she knew that one day, she would experience it all again.

Even in pain and unsure of her future, Amberly still tried to serve her clients and the nurses. She formed relationships with the nurses on her floor. Many opened their hearts to Amberly.

"I had a chair by my bed, and the nurses would come in exhausted. They poured their hearts out to me asking questions," she recalled. "I would listen and offer them suggestions, just like my grandmother did for me."

Focusing on the needs of others took her mind off her own pain.

Upon returning home, Amberly focused on the positive and brainstormed what she could do in her new normal. The obvious tasks were taking care of her children, attending therapies so she could continue to heal—but what could she do to provide for her family while suffering from chronic pain?

How bad was that pain? As mentioned before, her condition is dubbed the suicide disease. Some patients cannot tolerate the pain. Little can be done for management, so some resort to killing themselves. For Amberly, suicide was not an option. She had too much to live for. She was tough. She was a survivor. With grit and determination, she'd overcome this challenge too.

Not matter what she tried, it felt like fire ants were biting her leg day and night. The pain was deep in her nerves. She pursued every option from spinal stimulators, nerve blocks, ketamine infusions, taking dozens of homeopathic pills a day, opioids, alcohol, chakra balancing, and aura clearing. But nothing worked.

Despite her efforts to endure for her family, despair descended on her like a heavy blanket. Once in the best shape of her life, she found herself slipping into alcoholism, relying on wine to numb the pain. With each drink, the shame grew heavier weighing down her spirit as she struggled to cope with the overwhelming changes in her life.

She once believed that she had to carry the burden on her own. The thought of asking for help never crossed her mind as she convinced herself she wasn't worthy of it. "I have to push through the pain," she told herself, determined to struggle in silence, even though the weight of it all felt unbearable at times.

But pushing through the pain was not working for Amberly. She realized she needed to be radically honest with herself, fully accepting who she was and where she stood in her life. This acceptance became the turning point that allowed her to start taking purposeful action, fueled by grit. It wasn't just any grit, but one grounded in connection. Through this journey, she learned an important lesson: grit without connection is merely resistance but grit with connection is true resilience.

With this new mindset, Amberly endured dozens of surgeries, rebuilt her life, and got sober. Community and connection were her lifelines.

With her new outlook, Amberly started thinking about how to build a career despite living with chronic pain. Shifting her mindset to gratitude transformed her. She accepted her circumstances, held herself accountable, and connected with like-minded individuals who ignited her passion and perseverance.

Amberly reflects on how shifting her mindset toward gratitude became a transformative learning experience. She had to face the hard truth of being honest with herself and take full accountability for her life. It wasn't until she accepted her circumstances that she could begin taking the right steps forward. Connecting with a community of like-minded individuals was key to igniting her passion and perseverance. Her advice is simple yet powerful: focus on your why and activate the human spirit to drive your purpose.

During the interview, Amberly said the go-go-go mentality of modern society is a threat to our wellbeing. We must pause and listen to our bodies, knowing when to stop and plan times for rest and recovery. It's critical we take time to rest our minds and bodies.

"I've learned we must take care of ourselves," Amberly said. "I have something that I remind myself of every day when I'm feeling sad, anxious, or depressed."

Amberly calls it the Pacer methodology. It stands for perspective, acceptance, community, endurance, and rest. When there are days that she feels overwhelmed or anxious, she focuses on how she can shift her perspective.

The most important part of the PACER method according to Amberly is endurance.

Amberly emphasizes the importance of shifting your focus from the "how" or "what" you will do to understanding "why" you do it. She believes that by centering on your purpose, you activate the incredible power of the human spirit which is capable of far more than we often realize. The human spirit, she reflects, is powerful beyond measure when driven by a strong sense of purpose.

Through this process, Amberly has learned to ask for things simply. The power of asking inspired her to create her Unstoppable Life Mastermind Group.

She couldn't help but marvel at the incredible women who had come into her life. "These women are unbelievable," she said.. She prayed for faith-filled, driven women to come together and that's exactly what happened. "They are amazing!" she beamed. Whenever speakers came in, they knew just what to do, asking, "What do I need help with?" or "What do I need?" And without hesitation, those who could help stepped in. "That's what we do in this community—we support each other," she reflected, grateful for the bond they had formed.

Amberly learned asking for help takes courage. It's a lesson she discovered throughout her healing journey and rebuilding her career. Early on, she faced a big business decision when she met Trent Shelton. Knowing he had been part of a mastermind group that helped launch his career, Amberly decided to reach out for advice.

"I was thinking of joining this group, and I knew it had been instrumental for Trent, so I reached out to him, asking for his thoughts," she recalled. To her surprise, Trent shared his insight with her.

"I remember my husband saying, 'You just texted Trent Shelton?' And I said, 'Yeah, and he just saved me $25,000 because I dared to ask for his input.'" That simple act of reaching out made all the difference reinforcing Amberly's belief in the power of asking.

In addition to asking for help, Amberly talks about the importance of providing value to others. Do what you can to help those who can benefit from your advice, coaching, or a few minutes of your time.

Amberly shares a heartfelt story about one of her scholarship students in her mastermind group. This student consistently goes above and beyond to show her gratitude and support. "She has given every single one of my podcast episodes a shout-out," Amberly said. "When I'm about to speak on stage, without fail, she sends me a prayer specifically for that moment. She comments on every post, shares my content, and thanks me after every meeting we have." This unwavering appreciation and dedication deepen Amberly's desire to help the student even more.

Her mastermind is just one way Amberly helps women worldwide. Thousands turn out to see Amberly speak about resilience. She motivates her audiences to find resilience in their difficulties.

When you see her behind the curtain before her presentation, you would never know that she almost lost her leg and is in horrific pain.

Before Amberly gets on stage, she does push-ups. Right there in front of everyone backstage. It is her way of staying grounded, focused, and energized—no matter who is watching.

Amberly has also written a book called *True Grit and Grace. Turning Tragedy into Triumph*. The book focuses on Amberly's life and how it was forever changed but not without rich rewards. Through gratitude and self-care, she found the ability to walk again while living with the chronic pain of CRPS. Anyone who suffers from chronic pain must read Amberly's book. She knows what you are going through and can give you the tools to persevere.

"Nothing worked to stop my physical pain except for one thing," she said. "Only resilience."

Amberly reflects on how the healing process did more than just alleviate her physical pain. It helped her overcome the emotional burdens of depression, anxiety, fear, and self-doubt ultimately empowering her to not just survive but thrive in life. By switching her mindset to focusing on what she can do versus what she can't has helped her significantly. She does everything in her power to manage the pain. This includes living a healthy lifestyle with food and exercise.

Amberly will always have a difficult road to navigate through life. She says anyone in a similar situation needs to ask for help.

For years she tried to hide her pain and struggles believing she had to face everything on her own. "I tried to do it all by myself." But the moment she chose to stop carrying the burden alone, her life began to change.

Amberly discovered sharing her challenges with others revealed something unexpected. Many people were going through the same struggles. Whether it was about her entrepreneurial journey, launching a course, getting sober, or pursuing fitness goals, asking for help became the key to her growth. "When you reach out and open up," she realized, "you become unstoppable. It's when you do it together that you really start to grow."

When Amberly is not working to help other women, on stage, or writing, she hosts a podcast called "The Amberly Lago Show—Stories of True Grit and Grace". The podcast shares heartfelt stories of struggles and success to inspire listeners to keep their eyes on the prize and forge ahead.

"I remembered something my grandfather told me, Amberly recalled. 'You have a shovel in your hand. You can lean on it, pray for a hole, or start digging.' Right then and there, I realized I had a choice. I could either give up and give in to the pain or start digging and fighting to create something positive out of my circumstances."

Amberly continues to be a role model for women around the world by helping them in her workshops, speaking on stage, and through her book *True Grit and Grace. Turning Tragedy into Triumph.*

Amberly's story is an example of a woman who transformed tragedy into victory. She is proof that any challenge can be overcome with the support of others and the determination to believe in yourself.

Amberly's journey serves as an inspiration for all of us to not only overcome our challenges but use our experiences to help others. Her resilience, courage, and determination show that no matter how daunting the obstacles, we can rise above them and create a meaningful life for ourselves and those around us. So, let her story remind us that even in the darkest moments we can tap into the hope and strength within us to persevere. Let us embrace our true grit and grace knowing we can achieve anything we set our minds to. Let us also extend a helping hand to those around us offering support and compassion as we navigate journeys of resilience and growth. Together, we can make this world a more resilient and gracious place for all. Follow Amberly's example and reframe your struggles from being obstacles into opportunities for growth and self-discovery. Find joy in the journey, knowing every experience, good or bad, shapes us into the resilient beings we are meant to be. And most importantly, remember we are never alone.

"The one thing that we all have is resilience," said Amberly. "No matter if your circumstances have narrowed your possibility, you can still have the life that you have always imagined. A life of joy."

Now Amberly not only shares how resilience helps us overcome obstacles and challenges. In her new book, "Joy Through the Journey". She shares how to not only find joy through life's ups and downs but how to embrace the present moment, shift your mindset and tap into your joy.

Resources

- Amberlylago.com

Darlene Shortridge

Chapter 8
Never Give Up

"You'll never do a whole lot unless you're brave enough to try."

- Dolly Parton

Darlene Shortridge Mawhinney is not here today to tell her story. In September 2022, at the age of 56, she unexpectedly passed away. She was a wife, mother, grandmother, author, and entrepreneur.

I met Darlene through a women's Facebook group in 2020. I was embarking on writing my first book and posted a question about editing and publishing. A few women tagged Darlene, and by the next day Darlene and I were on the phone talking about my book and her company, 40 Day Publishing.

She was genuinely interested in what my book was about. She asked about my family, job, and goals. There was something authentic and caring about Darlene. I felt as if I had known her for years.

Within a day, I signed a contract with 40 Day Publishing to help me turn my manuscript into a polished, published book.

A few weeks after I shared my ideas for a second book with Darlene, (this one), she unexpectedly passed away.

I was in shock. I had never physically met her, but I felt I had known her through emails, phone calls, and social media.

Darlene was passionate about her faith, family, and writing. As I began to think about the stories I wanted to share in this book,

Darlene's was the first to come to mind. This book about women overcoming obstacles is perfectly fitting.

    I appreciate her husband, Dan, who shared her story in the way he thought Darlene would like it to be told. Darlene's story is about perseverance. Darlene's story is about never giving up facing the loss of nearly all her possessions. She kept her head up when the world's weight pulled her down. She found solutions when nearly everything failed.

    This is Darlene's story.

    Darlene Shortridge Mawhinney was the oldest of four siblings. From her first memories, her childhood was anything but normal. Her mother wasn't around to care for the children, and her father abandoned the family. Darlene's husband, Dan, says it was horrible for her.

    At just four years old, Darlene was thrust into the role of a mother figure for her younger siblings—a responsibility no child should have to bear. Her mother's self-centeredness left Darlene feeding, changing diapers of the other children. She even walked to the corner store by herself to buy milk because her mother refused to do it. It was a heavy burden for someone so young, but Darlene had no choice but to step up.

    Dan says Darlene told him stories about how her mom was verbally and physically abusive. "Darlene bore the brunt of her mother's wrath, thrust into a position of authority over the children, all while remaining subservient to a mother consumed by her own self-interest."

    Dan told me Darlene had blocked out most of her childhood memories from the ages of four to thirteen. This was a coping mechanism that helped her survive the trauma.

    Darlene's family moved frequently, never staying in one place for more than eight or nine months. Her life was a constant cycle of upheaval with changing schools, new apartments, and different men coming and going from the household.

    But Darlene had a strong relationship with Jesus Christ focusing on her faith to help her through her difficult childhood.

Her faith became her lifeline. Even as a young girl, she found solace in the belief that she still had a father figure to rely on—God.

As her relationship with Him grew, He filled her with truth and a sense of hope that sustained her through the challenges.

Lacking support and love from her family, the odds were against her. However, in her early teens, Darlene and one of her sisters went to live with their biological father. Before they left, her mom told her that her father didn't care about her or her sister.

"Darlene found out her dad wasn't the evil person as described for eight years," Dan said. "Her father had been financially supportive through the years but she was told otherwise by her mother."

For the first time in her life, Darlene flourished. No longer responsible for raising her younger siblings and suffering from abuse, Darlene found her voice.

"She had a gift for singing." Dan remembers. "She was a wonderful, wonderful vocalist. She pursued that through high school and even got a scholarship to go to college for vocal performance. She was starting to become Darlene."

Darlene got into college with a scholarship but discovered she didn't want to pursue a degree. She struggled financially and didn't love the structure of college.

After leaving school, she still sought an escape from her previous life. She met a man named Jim, and married when Darlene was only nineteen. Early in their marriage, there was a problem.

Darlene quickly realized Jim didn't want children. This was heartbreaking for her. Having kids had always been a part of her dream. She longed to be a mother and was determined to be a good one.

Darlene didn't leave, though. She spent six years trying to convince her husband to have a baby. Her conversations worked, and on May 30, 1992, Darlene gave birth to Jonna.

Darlene proved to be an excellent mom and devoted Christian. She was involved in church and worship ministry which gave her great joy. She also discovered her entrepreneurial side.

She took on a leadership role in worship, overseeing various groups, teaching the children's class, and organizing the curriculum. It was during this time that she began writing plays, musicals, and short stories. Darlene channeled her creativity into her newfound responsibilities.

Despite her success, Darlene was not happy in her marriage. Her husband did not support her goals and dreams, so she knew she had to leave. After sixteen years of marriage, Darlene and Jim divorced.

From an unhappy marriage to a single mom, Darlene's life was not what she expected but she had Jonna who mattered most to her. She worked full and part-time jobs while caring for her little girl. Darlene did what she could to survive.

And then she met Dan.

It was around St. Patrick's Day, March 2002, in Janesville, Wisconsin. Dan was the DJ for his cousin's annual corporate party. Dan's younger sister Dorrie was best friends with Darlene and invited her to the party.

"She came in the door very intentionally," Dan recalled. "She stopped halfway on the dance floor, looked up at me, and gave me this little wave and smile."

Dan recognized Darlene from church. He made his way over to say hi. Before she left, she told Dan, "We should get together sometime. I'd like to make you dinner."

Darlene called Dan the next day.

They sat down for dinner and ended up talking for six hours, diving into deep conversation right from the start. They covered everything—what they wanted to accomplish: their dreams, where they saw themselves in five years, and whether they wanted to have more children. It was all big, meaningful topics right out of the gate.

Dan had a very clear idea of the type of person he wanted to marry. He wanted somebody strong and independent. A woman whose Christian faith had been tried and was true. He also hoped to find a mate with an entrepreneurial bent. Darlene was all that and more. It didn't take long for Dan to recognize she was The One.

Two weeks later, Dan proposed. With a mix of excitement and nerves, he said, "I think we're meant to be together for the rest of our lives and I believe we should get married. So, will you marry me?" Her answer was immediate and full of joy, "Yes, I will." After a moment she asked, "Did you have a timeframe in mind?" Without missing a beat, he replied, "Yeah, I was looking at the calendar, and Sunday, the 21st of April, which is just a couple of weeks from now, seems like it would work out pretty well." They both smiled, knowing their future was falling perfectly into place.

A month after dating, Dan and Darlene married. The newlyweds wanted to put a priority on family life. Dan ran an entertainment business and decided to sell the company to his business partner. Dan took a variety of jobs including selling insurance.

A month after the wedding, they found out Darlene was pregnant. Planning for a baby while making ends meet was a struggle for them as it is for many families.

"What helped us through it all was that we were committed to being together, working together, and doing whatever we had to do," Dan recalled.

Discussions ensued about having Darlene stay home to raise the kids—especially during the early years. Money would be tight, but they were willing to make sacrifices for the sake of their children. Because they struggled financially, people were critical of Darlene being a stay-at-home mom. Dan formulated a good answer: "She's already working full time as a mom, a wife, a homemaker, and everything else."

As Darlene did the world's hardest and most important job, she started writing. It allowed her to be home with her children. It also provided her with an outlet for her creativity.

She came to Dan one day with a story swirling in her mind. "I feel like I'm supposed to write this story," she told him, her voice filled with excitement and uncertainty. He looked at her and simply said, "Okay, well, you should do it." His encouragement was all she needed to take the next step and put her thoughts into words.

Over the next few months, Darlene sat at her computer typing with tears rolling down her face as she poured her heart into the story.

Within a few months, Darlene had written close to 100,000 words. Never having created a manuscript before, she didn't know what to do with her story. After some research, she and Dan submitted it to Bethany House Publishing.

"We got the letter back from Bethany House in a thin envelope," Dan said. "We opened it, and it was a rejection letter. They said it wasn't the type of story they were looking for."

Despite the rejection, Darlene found a way for people to read her book. With limited resources and few options, Dan and Darlene went to an office store, made copies, bound the book with a spiral, and handed out forty copies to people they knew.

As the story began to circulate, they heard from people who had read it despite its rough, photocopied form. The feedback was overwhelming. Readers told them how wonderful the story was, how it had shifted their perspective on forgiveness and helped them overcome their own struggles. Yet they found themselves uncertain about what to do next.

After a while, life got busy and the book was set aside.

In 2008, Dan had been working for an automotive company. Finances were stable. The Mawhinneys could breathe.

Then Dan was unexpectedly laid off.

They found themselves in a difficult financial situation, forcing them to downsize and sell off whatever they could to cover their bills. Darlene started listing items on eBay to bring in extra money. Even then, one of their cars was repossessed leaving them with one vehicle.

Darlene was always optimistic and kept her head up despite their circumstances. In November of 2008, Dan was offered a job with a yellow pages company in Green Bay, Wisconsin. He accepted, and after downsizing even more and selling anything they could get rid of, they took a small van to Green Bay. A month after the move, Dan received frustrating news.

"It's not even December 1st," Dan recalled. "And I'm told the Green Bay office will be closed after the first of the year. This was after we had just moved on our dime."

Dan did what he could to make ends meet by picking up odd jobs. He bruised his knuckles with door-to-door sales and spent any free time selling family portraits. Through this hardship, Darlene's faith and love were unwavering.

He reflected on how strong his wife had been through it all. "She was a real trooper," he told me with admiration for her resilience. She understood that he was out there doing whatever needed to be done. Dan faced one challenge after another, trying to survive. Through it all, she stood by his side, supporting him every step of the way.

In the spring of 2010, the weary couple went to Darlene's favorite Mexican restaurant. They had to figure out how to provide for their family.

Dan glanced at Darlene, a thought suddenly crossing his mind. "What about your book?" he asked. "Do we believe in it? Do we believe the story has potential?" They both paused for a moment, reflecting on the power of the story they created. The real question was whether they would move forward with it or not. After a brief silence, they looked at each other and agreed. "Yes, let's make this happen."

Nearly broke, Dan and Darlene took their $4000 tax return and shopped for independent and traditional publishers. Little did they know, this decision would start a new chapter in their lives. They received offers on the book. Two from traditional sources and one from a subsidy publisher. They weighed the options and didn't want to give up their rights. Nor did they want the publisher to make significant changes. The Mawhinney's decided they preferred to have more control of the process. Choosing the subsidy publisher, they paid $3,895 of their $4,000 tax return. Ten months later, Darlene's book was published.

Darlene sold her book at speaking events. All seemed to be going well but...

Darlene and Dan hadn't anticipated the publisher would have complete control over the book's retail price. When they saw the paperback listed at $20.99, it felt too high. Darlene feared people wouldn't be willing to pay that much. To make matters worse, they were being charged $10 per copy for the paperbacks—a cost they hadn't expected. "We didn't know…we were blindsided by the whole thing," Dan admitted. Adding to their frustration, the marketing promised by the publisher never materialized leaving them disconnected from the process and unsure of how to move forward.

Time to explore other options.

Darlene researched independent publishing. What was it? How did it work? How much control would she, the author, have?

While the book was successful, Dan and Darlene still struggled. They downsized more. Eventually, the family hit a point where they couldn't afford to live in their current state. They moved to Alabama to live with Darlene's aunt and uncle. Not having the burden of paying rent or mortgage, they decided to use what little money they had to purchase back the rights to Darlene's book.

"For our story, we had to reach a point where we were completely unattached to anything material," Dan recalled. "It became all about our family. We had each other, we had our children, and that's all that mattered."

After procuring the rights to the book, Dan and Darlene taught themselves how to publish a book using the Amazon platform.

Dan learned formatting. Jonna redesigned the cover, and Dan wrote his own book, a restaurant training program.

Eventually, Dan got a job in Oklahoma City. They moved on Mother's Day weekend. During that time, they ran a Kindle Select promo of Darlene's book on Amazon. They decided to stop at a Starbucks hoping to take advantage of the free Wi-Fi and check on how the promotion was going. As Darlene pulled up the numbers, a look of disbelief crossed her face. "I don't know if this is right," she said, staring at the screen, "but it looks like we've hit 5,000 downloads, and the number keeps climbing."

By the end of the promotion, there were 30,000 downloads of her first book released on the Amazon platform. Once the free promotion was over, Darlene finally made money.

Encouraged by the dramatic sales, Darlene began working on her next book. Other authors noticed her seemingly quick rise to success. Some reached out asking questions about promotions, formatting, and marketing. For that first year, Darlene helped other fledgling authors for free. As the volume increased, someone suggested she could make money assisting other writers. That's how 40 Day Publishing was born. "We needed an easy-to-read book that was jam-packed with information," Dan explained.

The idea sparked a new direction for them. Why not help others become publishers themselves? By becoming independently published, authors could have full control over their pricing, rights, and distribution. This would free other authors them from the limitations Dan and Darlene experienced firsthand.

40 Day Publishing recently celebrated its tenth anniversary. Over that time, it has helped hundreds of authors publish multiple books.

Since Darlene is not here to share her wonderful wisdom and advice. I asked Dan what he imagined Darlene would say to those reading this book.

"Never give up. Never lose sight of the dream of where you want to go. Understand that adversity and failure will come and trials and tribulations are inevitable. These challenges happen to anyone chasing a dream whether it's becoming a wife, a mother, or a grandmother. But hold on to that dream, no matter what."

Darlene was bombarded with challenges throughout her life, yet she remained undeterred and strong.

"She was just an eternal optimist." Dan explained. "She said, 'Well, that didn't work, so let's try something different'. We kept getting knocked down, but she never gave up."

After years of struggling, Dan and Darlene finally achieved their dream of creating a full-time business together. They worked together every day. They chose their schedules so they could go where they wanted. They determined their income and achieved personal and professional success as soulmates.

"God brought us together. "-Dan Mawhinney

Resources

- www.40daypublishing.com

Meghan McNabb

Chapter 9

Love Yourself

'You don't have to struggle in silence. You can be un-silent. You can live well with a mental health condition, as long as you open up to somebody about it."

- Demi Lovato

At eighteen, Meghan McNabb embarked on a promising career in Canada's health and wellness industry. She became a personal health coach for the Purple Magic program, which she had benefited from as a teenager. Meghan's passion for assisting others on their health and weight loss journey was palpable, and her dedication did not go unnoticed.

At just 19 years old, Meghan excelled at her job, achieving one of the highest closing rates for sales for the organization across Canada. Whenever new participants joined the program, they sat down with her, and she personally guided them toward meeting their weight loss goals, ensuring they had the support needed to succeed.

Despite her professional achievements, the company faced financial difficulties and declared bankruptcy. Meghan played a key role in the daunting task of closing almost 300 locations nationwide. At twenty-one, facing uncertainty about her future, Meghan knew one thing for sure—her heart was set on continuing her career in the fitness industry. She quickly found her footing at one of Canada's premier gyms. Her career soared. Yet, beneath the surface of her professional success, personal turmoil simmered. She participated in the accelerated management training program and landed a role as an Assistant General Manager of a 4500-member gym. She had a personal trainer and was very successful at her job. But she was unhappy.

"My trainer said to me one day, Meghan, I think you have an eating disorder. My entire life changed."

Meghan knew she had an eating disorder but kept it hidden from everyone. Eventually, she decided to seek help and took a three-month leave of absence. During her outpatient program, she received treatment from a team of psychologists, a natural nutritionist, and a dietitian. Overcoming her disorder was challenging. It didn't fit into the typical categories. Meghan was diagnosed with an Eating Disorder Not Otherwise Specified (EDNOS). EDNOS is a condition in which sufferers cycle through bulimia, anorexia, and the abuse of diet supplements.

She took about ninety diet supplements a day. "I was restricting what I was eating," Meghan recalled. "I was only eating about 700 calories a day, and if I went over that threshold—even if it was just a couple of extra grapes—I would throw it up to keep myself in balance."

The intense therapy led Meghan to a painful but necessary realization—her career in the fitness industry, once a source of pride and joy, had become a toxic environment for her recovery. The unanimous advice from her therapists was to change careers—a daunting prospect that left her questioning her identity and future.

The prospect of switching careers left her feeling lost. She wondered what she would do next and who she would become. Everything she built her life around suddenly came to a grinding halt leaving her uncertain about the future.

She reflected on that difficult time, "I went through the program, and during that time, I met a boyfriend who turned out to be very abusive." She recalled the pain of that relationship. "It was probably the worst year of my life." The memory of that dark chapter still lingers.

Meghan went through the eating disorder program to get healthy and was focused on her future. Shortly after her treatment, Meghan met a man. They dated. Unfortunately, it was far from a healthy relationship.

"The man I met tried to groom me to become a madame, Meghan said. "He couldn't convince me to sell myself, but he tried to convince me to sell other girls."

Meghan couldn't shake the discomfort her boyfriend's idea of a "career" brought her. It clashed with everything she believed. In a pivotal moment of clarity, she decided to redefine her life. She chose to stand up and fight against everything her boyfriend represented.

With quiet strength, she recalled, "I ended up rescuing four women from trafficking."

That choice at that moment wasn't just about defiance—it was about reclaiming her purpose and making an impact far more significant than she ever imagined.

Meghan's boyfriend appeared to run an underground human trafficking operation. She says he and his cronies would bring vulnerable women to a cottage, confiscate their money, and try to convince them to sell their bodies to earn it back. Meghan's boyfriend wanted her to oversee these women and persuade them to prostitute themselves.

One weekend, Meghan's boyfriend brought a young woman and her boyfriend to her cottage. The woman confided in Meghan. She had a three-year-old child and felt deeply uncomfortable with her boyfriend, who was there with them. "She told me she needed to get away." However, while Meghan was concerned for the woman's safety, her boyfriend had a different agenda. "He told me I should talk to her and convince her to do some work," Meghan added, the implication clear and troubling.

Meghan reports she knew the business was questionable but didn't fully realize until that moment what her boyfriend's "business" was about.

Meghan knew she had to act. She told the woman to get in her car and they drove an hour and a half together to the nearest bus station.

RISING ABOVE

From there, the woman boarded a bus headed to a location sixteen hours away far from the life she was trying to escape. Six months later, Meghan received a message from the woman on Facebook. She and her son had started a new life and were incredibly thankful. For Meghan, it was a profoundly eye-opening moment that changed her perspective forever.

"I already had an inkling this was happening because of the conversations he kept having with me," Meghan explained. "He would say, 'You have lots of friends. You're a beautiful woman. You attract beautiful women around you.' He'd tell me it's easy for women to make money—they can start their careers this way. He was very good at manipulation."

There was no way out. If a captured couple ran out of money, they'd have to pay Meghan's boyfriend for a ride back to the city. That debt would then be added to what they already owed him. When the boyfriend couldn't pay—usually because drugs were involved—the focus would shift to the girlfriend, leaving her vulnerable to trafficking.

After freeing the woman, Meghan knew she was in danger. She didn't know what to do. Her life was out of control. She fell back into what she could control: food. The eating disorder reared its ugly head.

Meghan's boyfriend had become a master at manipulating her. Things escalated to the point where he even tried to break her hand, a sign of the chaos and control he exerted over her life. They shared a cell phone, so Meghan had to hide her messages, carefully deleting them after each conversation. Her friend was the only person she could confide in, the only one who knew what was really happening behind closed doors.

"One day, I locked myself in the bathroom," Meghan remembered. "I told my friend that I can't do this anymore. I just wanted to curl up till I died. She said I needed to get in a car, leave, and come to her house. And I did."

Sneaking around the apartment, Meghan packed up what she could while her boyfriend was away. She got in her car and fled.

Meghan was terrified. At the same time, she felt a sense of reassurance. When she returned to the area, she began hearing stories about her ex which involved other girls. Determined to help, she started warning them about what had happened to her. One day, she met a girl with a similar story. "He had even changed his name with them," Meghan said. She looked the girl in the eye and said, "You need to get away from him right now, and you need to tell all your friends too."

A few years later, Meghan's boyfriend was arrested for human trafficking.

Meghan says it showed her how scary the world can be and how she spent her life seeking unhealthy relationships. She says she had a fear of food, expressed as an eating disorder, and a fear of men.

Over time, Meghan noticed a troubling pattern in her life—she kept attracting unhealthy relationships. It forced her to take a step back and recognize the importance of being cautious about the people she allowed into her life. Reflecting on her vulnerability, she realized in her desperation for love, she surrounded herself with toxic individuals. Deep down, she understood her choices stemmed from not loving herself, leading her to do things she otherwise wouldn't have.

"I just wanted people to love me," Meghan said. "And you end up doing things because you don't love yourself."

Through intense work, Meghan has been free of her eating disorder for ten years.

Now, fully recovered, she has come to understand that vulnerability was an integral part of who she was. Every decision she made was for her well-being and no longer shaped by the need to please others. Her mission had become clear: to fall in love with herself and live authentically on her terms.

With the past behind her, Meghan returned to work in Ontario.

Her role involved connecting business owners with mentors who had succeeded in leadership positions. She quickly fell in love with the concept. Scaling an idea into a thriving business captivated her and business planning became a passion. Her interest grew so much that she pursued a post-graduate degree in social media marketing eager to expand her knowledge and skills in the field.

RISING ABOVE

Meghan went on to work for a web filtering company that protects users on the internet from porn, child trafficking, and human trafficking. She ran fifteen regions by herself and loved it. But Meghan knew she wanted more.

In 2018, Wildly Digital was born. It is a firm dedicated to helping businesses navigate the ever-changing digital landscape. Meghan and her friend from grad school partnered to launch the industry and they've thrived ever since. Wildly Digital serves as the operational management hub for all things digital assisting businesses with start-ups, marketing, branding, business operations, and even their company's overall energy and culture.

Meghan, now a mom, is extremely passionate about helping parents understand how the internet works so they may protect their children.

According to the Centers for Disease Control and Prevention, the number of suicides in females aged fifteen to twenty-four increased eighty-seven percent over the past twenty years. Among males aged fifteen to twenty-four, the number of suicides rose by thirty percent over that same time. A recent study from Facebook found Instagram to have harmful effects among a portion of its millions of young users—particularly teenage girls. Findings indicated that Instagram makes body image issues worse for one in three teenage girls. And among teenagers who reported suicidal thoughts, six percent in the U.S. traced back to Instagram.

Meghan spent most of her childhood and young adult life trying to recognize her self-worth and feel loved. She is not alone in that struggle. Millions of people struggle with eating disorders, body dysmorphia, and being in abusive relationships. She has advice for anyone going through a similar situation.

"Find the love in yourself. And if you don't know how to find that love in yourself, find something you love and lean into that. You don't have to be a religious person, but there is a higher power that exists in all of us. It's just listening to that voice and that voice fully loves you.
"

Organizations like the National Domestic Violence Hotline offer resources and assistance to those experiencing abuse. These include a 24/7 hotline, safety planning, and referrals to local resources for shelter, legal support, and counseling. It is crucial to remember that seeking help is not a sign of weakness but a brave step towards reclaiming one's life.

Meghan's story is a powerful testament to determination. It's a journey that took her from the depths of personal struggle to the heights of courage and empowerment. Despite her challenges, her experiences illuminate the difficult path to recovery and demonstrate the strength it takes to stand up for oneself and others. Through this journey, Meghan discovered her true purpose which was inspiring those who have lost their way.

Had Meghan not acted when she did, she and the women she saved from her boyfriend's grip might not be here today to share their stories. They might not have had the chance to live safe, healthy lives or help others understand online predators' lurking dangers.

Because Meghan listened to her inner voice, she escaped, healed, and now embraces her most significant responsibility: being a mother.

If you are a victim of trafficking or know someone who is, please call National Human Trafficking Hotline 888-373-7888.

Resources

- www.wildlydigital.com
- Fully Nourished Podcast
- Mel Robbind Podcast
- Natal chart: https://cafeastrology.com/
- The patterns app https://play.google.com/store/apps/details?id=com.thepattern.app
- The Desire Map - Danielle Laporte
- Dare to Lead - Brent Brown
- Outliers - Malcom Gladwell
- 7 Habits of Highly Effective People - Sean Covey
- The 4 Hour Work-Week - Tim Ferris

John O'Hurley and Alison Maloni.
Living my dream in New York, interviewing fascinating people.

Chapter 10
You are Enough

"You either walk inside your story and own it, or you stand outside your story and hustle for your worthiness."

-Brene Brown

I walked down the long hallway wearing a perfectly fitted red dress, hair so stiff with hairspray that a category five hurricane wouldn't move it, and makeup set for the camera lights. As I carefully put one foot in front of the other to try not to fall in my high heels that had been damaged earlier in the escalator, my point-of-view shifted. It was if I was detached from my body watching from a corner near the ceiling. I wouldn't call it an out-of-body experience, but it felt like it. I can still see my form from behind, going to the studio, laptop and notebook in one arm, coffee in the other hand.

It wasn't the vision of me walking down the national news studio hallway, but the feeling I had and the thoughts running through my head. Oh my God, I made it. How the heck did I get here? How did a broken and insecure child with an eating disorder who was told that she was meant to be behind the camera, not in front of it, get here?

When I was just 23 years old, I worked as a general assignment reporter at a local television station. I was also a producer and assignment editor. In small markets, you're a jack of all trades. It wasn't unusual to produce a show and then run out the door to do a live shot in a 12-hour day. I didn't care. I loved it, and I knew you did this to earn your place in a bigger market.

One day, the news director called me into her office. She looked me straight in the eye and said, *"Alison, you are a great producer. Some people are meant to be in front of the camera, and others should be behind it. You are much better behind the scenes."*

I held back tears, smiled, and told her I'd keep trying to be a better reporter. But as soon as I left, I rushed to the bathroom and let the tears flow. That moment crushed me. All I wanted was to be a reporter; I had just been told to give up. Those old doubts crept right in: *Maybe I'm not good enough.*

But something clicked. Maybe it was anger. Perhaps it was determination. I wiped the tears and told myself, *"No. I won't let her tell me what I'm capable of. I'm not giving up."* A few months later, I gave her my notice. I was off to a bigger market. And let me tell you, that smile did not leave my face for days.

If I had listened to her, I never would have gone to Providence, where I worked for a wonderful news director named Gary Brown. Unlike my former boss, he told me that I was meant to work in the network news. And 15 years later, he was right.

I share that story with young women all the time. Words are powerful. If someone tells you you aren't good enough, let it fuel you, not break you. Let it be the fire that lights your drive.

I dreamed about this moment as a little girl but never imagined it would happen—especially since I was in my forties and had been out of the television industry for fifteen years.

But there I was, about to sit at the anchor desk and do what I loved doing.

I pretended I wasn't nervous, but my heart tried to pound its way out of my chest. No matter how much water I drank, my mouth felt like cotton. Throw up or pass out—my body urged me to pick one.

The crew took their places. Lights were adjusted. I skimmed my notes. This was it. What would people think of me? Will they hate me? Will they criticize my dress? My face? Will the network fire me? Am I past my prime?

Am I good enough?

That question echoed in my mind on repeat.

It wasn't a new question. In fact, that pesky mantra invaded my life at the age of four, on March 15, 1980.

I arrived home from preschool and walked through the front door. Immediately I noticed my father lying on the couch with its blue floral design—a detail I remember vividly, even to this day.

His hand on his forehead caused my gut to clench. Something bad happened. Hoarse voice barely above a whisper, my dad gave me the worst news a preschooler could receive—my mother had died. I didn't fully grasp what 'death' meant so I stormed upstairs to my bedroom and cried. The rest is a blur. I don't remember her funeral or much of the days that followed.

Fortunately, I have a few memories of my beautiful mom. I remember her making applesauce in the kitchen and singing 'You are my Sunshine' to me. When I was three, she always took me to the park. My favorite part of our adventure was going down the slide.

During our last Christmas together, I got a Sit 'n Spin from Santa. I couldn't have been more excited. If you are under the age of forty-five you probably don't know what I'm talking about. But it was all the rage in the early 80s and every child wanted one. It does exactly what it says. You sit and spin. That Christmas morning in our beautifully decorated colonial home in Massachusetts, I spun around and around despite Mom warning me to stop because I'd just finished breakfast and might get sick. I neglected to listen to my mom and kept spinning.

And sure enough, I threw up all over my one-piece Christmas pajamas. Turns out she was right. Aren't moms always right?

I remember the look on her face—the look all moms give—the "told you so" look. She quickly scooped me up and bathed me. With a fresh set of clean pajamas, I was back in the living room with my mom, dad, and dalmatian, Lucky.

Lurching forward to return to that Sit 'n Spin, I got the look. Again. It was stern, but I could see the smile behind it. This time I listened to her. Little did I know it was the last time I would sit under the Christmas tree with her.

Three months later, my mom died from lymphoma at the age of thirty-five.

My dad, a Marine and Vietnam veteran, faced the challenge of raising a young daughter on his own. Needing help, he hired a nanny to care for me. That's how I met Nanci.

I recall telling her in a firm, but scared tone, that she was not my mother. I liked her but I didn't understand what her role was. My mom just died and now there's this new woman here. Living in my house? Taking care of me? So much happened in a short amount of time.

It didn't take long for me to come to love Nanci. She was young, pretty, and a motherly figure. I was attached to Nanci's hip and thought of her as a version of my mom. I craved love, attention, and family. I just wanted to be loved.

Six months later, my dad decided to remarry. This woman's children were grown, and she had no interest in raising a young child. I can't speak for her, but I had always assumed she didn't want me. And just like that, Nanci was taken out of my life.

Within six months, I lost my mother and Nanci.

My mom had taught me how to say my prayers before bed. I would start by asking God to bless my mom, my dad, and everyone important in my life. After asking for blessings, I asked God why He took my mom away from me. Why did He take Nanci? What did I do wrong? Was it because I wasn't good enough?

I was so young back then; I didn't understand the ways of God.

Those six months passed by like a whirlwind and I blocked out my dad's new relationship. Then he sold the house, taking away yet another piece of familiarity.

We moved into his new wife's house and I hated it. I recall a lot of fighting. When that happened, I hid in this old, smelly attic. It was dusty and smelled like mildew but it was the only place I could escape the loud yelling. I remember telling myself that when I became a mom, I would never yell like that in front of my children to the point where they were scared to come out of their rooms.

Much of my early childhood was spent in fear. I waited for the inevitable screaming matches between dad and stepmother. One of the worst moments happened when we were at Cape Cod. My stepmother kicked my dad and I out of the car and left us on the side of the road. We had to hitchhike back to the house. Why did she do that? Why would she leave us stranded?

Again, my young brain assumed it had been something I did or didn't do. I had to figure this out and make myself better…whatever that meant.

It came to a point that my maternal grandparents realized my living situation wasn't healthy. Rumors of my dad moving us to Europe circulated.

My grandparents discussed this with my father, who decided it was best for them to raise me. So, I went to live with them and he continued his life with his new wife. He never visited, and I never went to see him.

My dad fought in Vietnam and has since told me he had been diagnosed with PTSD (Post Traumatic Stress Disorder). I am not writing this to discredit him or place blame. I won't ever know how PTSD affects one's ability to make life decisions. I love my dad and always will, no matter what.

Within a year, I had lost my mother, my nanny, my house, and my father.

I was living with my grandparents by the age of five. I shared a room with my grandmother and had a small playroom on the porch. My grandparents were devastated over the loss of my mom but thrilled to have me with them.

I attended the Catholic school my mom wanted me to go to before she died. Considering everything that happened, I was a well-adjusted child. I did well in school, had many friends, and enjoyed life.

My grandparents were terrific and did their best to care for a young, energetic little girl. But when I turned eight, my grandmother's health started to deteriorate. She was never the same after my mom died. As a mother, I can't imagine losing a child and what that does to you. Just as I had watched my mom get sick with cancer, I witnessed my grandmother suffer from a stroke. She was bedridden, and a few years later, died of a heart attack.

By the age of eight, I had lost my mom, nanny, house, dad, and grandmother.

My grandfather aged quickly. Caring for me became too much. My mom's sister and her husband took me in. They had no children of their own and welcomed me with open arms. My aunt had spent years enduring surgeries and treatments hoping for a child but it never happened. Maybe, in some way, my mom was working alongside God to bring me to her.

And off I went—to a new home, town, and school. I was getting good at moving. I hoped this would be the last one. Was it possible I'd found security and stability at last?

What none of use were prepared for, was how all the loss I experienced at a such a young age would affect me in the future.

By the time I was nine, I adjusted well (once again) to a new school and household. It was awkward explaining my story to kids I met because I had to share what happened to my mom and grandmother. I also felt the need to explain why my dad wasn't in the picture.

Somewhere along the way, I decided I didn't want to go to school anymore so I faked an illness. I liked school, but I feared something would happen to my aunt while I was in the classroom—away from home.

For the first time in my life, I was happy and felt safe. And in my elementary school aged mind, I formed a correlation: when I was at school those I loved were taken from me. If I were to keep going to school, it was only a matter of time before my aunt would die or leave. Everyone else in my life had.

I was terrified of being abandoned. The only time I felt safe was when I was with my aunt and uncle. I needed to be with them constantly.

Eventually, I had to return to school. My feelings of impending loss festered, and I hated myself for shirking my responsibility to keep my family safe.

While away from home for seven hours a day, I felt as if everything in my life was out of my control. Something had to give, and I needed to control something—and that something was my eating.

I remember that day like it was yesterday. I was playing outside with a neighborhood friend when he looked at me and said, "Alison, you are fat."

That was all I had to hear. Words have power. They can do so much good and yet so much damage. You never know what someone has gone through or is going through. If I hadn't been through the loss and abandonment, maybe I could have brushed it off.

Fat.

Because of his stated observation, I saw myself as fat.

Those words stayed with me. And they stay with me today.

After he pronounced that over me, every time I looked in the mirror I saw a fat, fat girl.

I hated looking at myself. But when I did, I examined every inch of my body with a critical eye. I wore clothes I hoped made me look skinny. I prayed to God every night to not let me be fat. Please, God, make me skinny. I threw a penny in a fountain and my wish was, be thin. Anytime I had an opportunity to pray or wish to be skinny, I asked for it.

I cut back on my eating and exercised in my room every night in addition to my dance classes. My aunt and uncle noticed my weight loss. They also noticed I stopped eating.

Dinnertime became a constant battle. They begged me to eat.

I went from being healthy to skin and bones. My aunt and uncle struggled with what to do, so they sought therapy for me. I went every week for a very long time. I finally started eating again and gained weight.

Through therapy, my therapist and I explored the deep-rooted issues of loss, abandonment, and self-esteem stemming from those early tragedies. I'm not sure I'd be here today if my aunt and uncle hadn't gotten me the help I needed. And while I'd love to say I've completely overcome those struggles, the truth is I still battle with body image. The negative thoughts crept back a few years ago and they still surface from time to time. More than I would like.

But therapy made a difference. It helped me heal and find a healthier path. From there, I began to thrive. I graduated high school with honors, went on to college, and launched my career.

Occasionally I visited my father but it's never been smooth sailing. I've come to terms with that.

Working in the television industry, I married at twenty-six, had three beautiful daughters, and started a public relations business. Life was great. But unfortunately, our marriage took a difficult turn and I was divorced at the age of forty-one.

I was a single mom trying to figure out a new life. And while I was doing that, my confidence was sky high. I felt really good about myself. I was terrified about how I was going to pave my own way, but I was strong and ready to take on the world.

In 2018, that slowly changed. I say slowly because looking back, I can see all the moments when I started to feel I wasn't skinny enough, pretty enough, or outgoing enough. I just felt... not enough. I was trying to fit into this new life, adapting to new friends and a different lifestyle. I wasn't myself anymore and it was exhausting. All I wanted was to be liked and loved. God, I was so desperate to become the person I thought I needed to be. It was like being right back in the mindset of that nine-year-old—only this time, it was worse.

It so happened my worst fears came true. A relationship I had placed above all else ended suddenly. Our wedding was called off. I was heartbroken, nearly broke, and felt more abandoned than ever.

I put that relationship before my children, friends and family. I was not the Alison my parents brought me up to be. I was not the Alison my mom in heaven is watching over. However, had I stayed in that situation, I would have lost everything.

I learned when we don't take ourselves out of certain situations, God will.

Feeling abandoned, alone, and broke, I curled up on my floor at night sobbing until the tears ran out. I had tried to rebuild my life, career, heart, and self-confidence. But I only had ten dollars to my name.

In order to buy groceries, I borrowed money from my parents. I lost weight again and everything seemed to be spiraling out of control.

On the outside, I presented as if I had my life together. I posted on social media regularly. I went out with friends. I even made a point to share positive quotes.

Yet, I was the biggest imposter on social media.

But I was dying inside. I wanted everyone to believe my life was great and I was doing wonderful. And yet—I knew I had to work on myself. I had to find me again.

What I've learned through therapy and self-relfection is that you can't truly build a career or relationships until you love yourself. And that takes a lot of work—years of work.

I was determined never to feel like that again. I read all the books I could find, listened to podcasts, rebranded my business, wrote articles and blogs to increase my visibility, focused on being present in my children's lives, and went to therapy. For once, I focused on what I wanted in life and what I wanted in my career. I focused on me.

And slowly, things started to fall into place.

TV appearances. More clients. A new relationship. More laughter. Real, deep, belly-aching laughter—the kind that makes you cry. It had been so long since I felt that.

Over time I changed. I no longer compared myself to other women. I no longer worried about being cheated on.

I could finally be myself.

I was, about to submit this book to my publisher for final edits when life threw me an unexpected curveball—one that would change the ending of this chapter. Just like Katie in the first chapter, my life suddenly took a turn, and it wasn't a good one.

As you probably know by now, I'm an open book when it comes to my life. But this time, I won't be sharing the details. Some things are too private, too painful. Sometimes we need to handle things quietly, behind the scenes without an audience.

So why am I even mentioning this if I'm not going to share the details?

Because I couldn't end this book with the perfect, wrapped-in-a-bow conclusion I had planned.

The truth is, there is no perfect life, no perfect ending, no perfect job, and no perfect partner.

Life is full of bumps in the road. Sometimes, massive potholes. But you find a way through. You navigate. You seek help. You pray.

The past forty-eight years of ups and downs, triumphs, and losses have taught me this: you must feel the pain, process it, and then take the next step forward—no matter how unsteady it feels. Because life doesn't stop. Responsibilities don't pause. And neither do our dreams.

Back to that long hallway I was walking down to anchor the network news for the first time. Despite everything I had overcome, despite all the healing I had done, those old, familiar questions still echoed in my mind.

Was I enough?

Turns out, I was.

I made it through the newscast with my co-host, Bob Sellers, who also became a wonderful coach to me. We launched two shows and have been on Newsmax for over six years.

I won't say those awful thoughts don't creep into my head. In fact, as I write this, I've been battling them all day. Perimenopause can really mess with your mental and physical fitness. (Maybe that's my next book.)

But here's the difference: When those thoughts arise, I change the story.

I tell myself I will have a great newscast. My viewers will like me. My business will thrive. My career will grow. My life will be good.

You'd be surprised at the outcome when you change how you think.

To that little girl and that forty-three-year-old woman who thought she wasn't enough—

Darling, you are more than enough.

Resources

- AlisonMayCommunications.Com
- You are a Badass
- Ask Gary Vee
- Millionaire Success Habits
- Calm Down Podcast

Conclusion

The women in this book were extraordinarily brave and courageous enough to share their stories and missions with the world. As I compiled hours of interviews, certain common themes emerged transcending age, background, and geography. Many of these women turned to faith to navigate through immense pain and challenges. For some, a steadfast faith saw them through while others who previously lacked a connection to God found newfound strength in prayer and reading scriptures during their darkest moments.

Life is about choices. Oftentimes, those choices are not easy or clear. The women featured in this book had every reason to succumb to despair, whether through suicide, alcohol, or negative thoughts. Yet, they chose to fight. They emerged from the darkness, adjusted their mindsets, sought help, and dedicated themselves to uplifting others. From aiding women in abusive relationships and sharing critical knowledge on health and wellness to saving children's lives both in and out of the classroom, these women chose to see the light and make a positive impact.

Because of their choices, people are alive today. I am honored to have met Darlene, Katie, Megan, Samantha, Amy, Amberly, Rebecca, Scarlett, and Sarah and share their incredible stories with you. My hope is that their experiences remind you of the resilience of the human spirit and inspire you to overcome any obstacles in your own life. May these womens' journeys of faith, strength, and determination remind us we are never alone, no matter what we face.

Acknowledgments

This book would not be possible without the unwavering support and constant uplifting conversations with my husband, Jon. I often wanted to stop writing or questioned my decision to write this—especially my story. Yet he encouraged me to keep going and change my mindset. I honestly don't think I would have pushed through if it wasn't for him.

To my three beautiful girls. I am so thankful for your hugs and patience. I am unsure how often I said, "I can't…I'm writing," or "Can you wait because I have to get this done." I am so blessed to have you and am a better person because of you. McKenna, Addison, and Hannah thank you for loving me unconditionally and your resilience during dark times. I love you all so much.

Mom and Dad, thank you for always checking in on me and supporting me during the hardest times in my life. You have been my lifeline from a young age, and I can't thank you enough.

Newsmax, thank you for giving me the opportunity of a lifetime. It has been my dream since I was a little girl to be on network news and because of you, I am there. Thank you for allowing me to do what I love while I get to be a mom, run a business, and write. Thank you for allowing me to share stories the world needs to hear.

www.ingramcontent.com/pod-product-compliance
Lightning Source LLC
Chambersburg PA
CBHW061729070526
44583CB00024B/3072